A GOOD MAN

IS HARD TO FIND

A GOOD MAN

IS

HARD TO FIND

Jo Lynne Pool

THOMAS NELSON PUBLISHERS
Nashville • Atlanta • London • Vancouver

Published in Nashville, Tennessee, by Thomas Nelson, Inc.

The Bible version used in this publication is the THE NEW KING JAMES VERSION. Copyright © 1979, 1980, 1982, 1990, Thomas Nelson, Inc., Publishers.

Library of Congress Cataloging-in-Publication Data

Pool, Jo Lynne, 1948-
    A good man is hard to find / Jo Lynne Pool.
        p.   cm.
    ISBN 0-7852-8166-5 (pbk.)
    1. Mate selection—Religious aspects—Christianity.   2. Christian women—Conduct of life.   I. Title.
BV835.P66   1995
248.4—dc20   94-24069
                                                        CIP

Printed in the United States of America

16 17 18 19 20   02 01 00

Contents

Preface

Let's first establish that it _can_ be done. Don't listen to the world's voice, Satan's voice, or your own voice mumbling in the background that "I'm never going to get married," "If it were going to happen, it would have happened by now," or "I don't know if I can wait until it happens." Tell the devil, the world, and yourself to quiet down. It's time now to listen to God . . . first and foremost, when He talks directly to you, and second, in this case, to listen to testimony from a woman who has been exactly where you are now, but who knows firsthand what God can do.

It was never my intention to write a book, but the Lord Himself planned otherwise. One night, He woke me out of a deep sleep and gave me the outline for the book you are about to read, complete with parts, chapter titles, and subheads. I have changed nothing from His original outline. Every night thereafter, for a period of more than five months, it was as though He commanded "Write," and words, phrases, and concepts bubbled up and flowed onto paper. I wrote each night, sometimes all night, as He opened up Scriptures, verses, and revelations. My background is not that of a writer; God is the literal author of this book. I'm only the vessel He used. Every word in this book has been prefaced by prayer and lived by experience . . . not only mine, but that of dozens of other Christian women of various ages, ethnic backgrounds, and religious denominations, whose testimonies are included as verification that it is never too late, and that regardless of their situations, God heard and answered the sincere cries of their hearts.

I know that if you are currently in the "holding phase" of waiting for a mate, these seem to be empty words, the things that happen to everybody else, but never to you. Well, stop it, right now. You must never again listen to the negative "I can't . . . it won't . . ." voice of the evil one. God has made you a stronger woman than that. And I am here to try to make your exciting journey a little easier to understand. If you take these words to your heart and put them into practice in your life, your trip can be a good deal smoother and a lot more rewarding. Now let's get started.

Part 1

YOU AND GOD'S PLAN

"The solid foundation of God stands."

2 Timothy 2:19

Chapter 1

It Can Be Done God's Way

If you've been a Christian for any length of time and you are a single woman, you have heard the voices of your friends and acquaintances, saved and unsaved alike, suggesting to you both subtly and openly that God's way does not really work . . . You've got to get out there and help Him along, or worse yet, just discard all that biblical nonsense and do it your own way.

I have been there, I've also heard them, and I am here now to tell you that "God is not a man, that He should lie" (Num. 23:19). His way is the only way that works in every area of your life, and His hands are not tied in the arena of romance. It was His plan and His design that men and women should be paired as husband and wife. He doesn't find it strange that you desire a mate, and as you'll see further along in this book, He has worked many notable romantic miracles and will continue to do so. He is perfectly capable of delivering a man to you seemingly out of nowhere, but there are things that *you* can do to make His task a bit easier. That's what this book is all about. As with everything else, God has a plan for your life in the area of marriage. Try not to set up roadblocks to His plan. God wants to work with you, in you, and through you to meet not only the needs in your life, but also your hopes, dreams, and deepest desires. Psalm 37:4–5 states that you are to "Delight yourself also in the LORD, and

He shall give you the desires of your heart. Commit your way to the LORD, trust also in Him, and He shall bring it to pass." God is on your side, but you've got to give Him a chance; you've got to do it His way.

ONCE UPON A TIME

Of course I have a testimony of God's power on the mating front, or how else could I have the conviction to write this book and to know whereof I speak?

I was thirty-two years old when I finally committed my life to Christ, for good. I first received the Lord at age fifteen in a revival meeting in my little hometown in Texas, but I went off to college in New York City and encountered the world headlong. I didn't consciously walk away—I just forgot everything I knew. I married an exciting, worldly older man of twenty-seven when I was twenty years old. The marriage produced two lovely, brilliant children (Yes, I can say that honestly, even though I'm their mom), whom I ended up raising alone. Several moves and much trauma later, I found myself and my kids newly transplanted to Houston. Although I hadn't set foot in a church in years, I decided to inquire about a church to attend, figuring that would be as good a place as any to meet new friends and maybe to find a new man. The "chance" recommendation of an acquaintance led me to a service on an Easter morning, and several visits later, to salvation and a personal knowledge of the Lord Jesus Christ. Little did I guess that I would not find a man, but rather, *The* Man—Jesus Himself.

I plunged wholeheartedly into my church, and single-mindedly into Christ. After eight years of raising my children alone, I had all but given up hope of finding a suitable husband, especially since now as a Christian, I had been given a whole new set of criteria to look for. No longer could he be merely good-looking and rich; now he had to be a Christian, and not just that—He had to be a born-again, spirit-filled

Christian who prayed fervently and followed the Lord in all his ways.

I thought it was impossible that I'd ever meet the right man, especially since I didn't even know any dateable Christian men. However, if you believe in the power of Christ, never say never since "with God all things are possible" (Mark 10:27). At age thirty-eight, I was married to the Christian man whom God had specially prepared for me. I met and married my husband during the same time period that *Time* magazine raised a huge statistical furor citing that a woman of forty (or close to it) had a better chance of being killed by a terrorist than she had of marrying. The way we met was, in itself, a miracle, which I'll describe later. But before I was ready to either recognize or accept what the Lord had in store for me in marriage, there were changes I had to make, and attitudes and activities I had to come to terms with. Like many people, I possess a hard head and a questioning nature, but fortunately, God really does know our hearts. When we are truly ready and have decided in our hearts to follow Him all the way, the doors we want to see opened will swing wide. All we have to do is walk through.

NOW—WHAT DOES GOD SAY?

As with everything in life, God lays down specific instructions—not just guidelines, but rules—for the Christian woman on how to view herself, and what to look for in a mate. I'll give an overview for you, the Christian woman, here—we'll get into the details concerning both you and your mate-to-be in the chapters that follow. For now, get your Bible and let's check out what the Word says:

About You
- Proverbs 31:10. "Who can find a virtuous wife? For her worth is far above rubies."
- Proverbs 18:22. "He who finds a wife finds a good thing, and obtains favor from the LORD."

- 1 Corinthians 7:2. "Let each man have his own wife, and let each woman have her own husband."
- John 15:7. "If you abide in Me, and My words abide in you, you will ask what you desire, and it shall be done for you."
- Matthew 13:45. "Again, the kingdom of heaven is like a merchant seeking beautiful pearls, who, when he had found one pearl of great price, went and sold all that he had and bought it."

"How does all this relate to me?" you ask. For the answer, pay attention to what the Bible is stating. God does not speak in riddles. He makes Himself perfectly clear. Let's look at the truths contained in these Scriptures, since they are central to the message contained in this book.

If you are a virtuous (Christian) woman, your worth is of greater value even than rubies.

If a man found a pearl of great value that he was seeking, he would consider it worth his while to let go of all his possessions in order to own it. A pearl, though truly exquisite in its beauty, is still of lesser value than the rare and extraordinary ruby. The Bible says a virtuous woman has value above rubies, that is, your value as a Christian woman is above both that of a "pearl of great price" and of rubies. You, dear Christian lady, are a precious gem, a woman of great value—you are definitely a prize to be sought after, of great worth to the man who finds you.

Pay attention to the word "find" in Proverbs, chapters 18 and 31. It is there for a reason; it is up to the man to do the "finding," the discovering. It is not for you to go out and hunt down your own guy. The world will tell you there are millions of hungry women out there looking for one good man and that you must join the fray. Get out there, find one, fight for him. You've heard the whole routine.

But the Bible says "he" shall find *you*. Since when does a pearl get up out of its shell or a ruby loose itself from the earth and go on a quest for someone to give itself to? The seeker knows it's there waiting for him alone to find this gem of great beauty and worth. He would run away if it came up and tapped him on the toe.

God's ideal for every man and every woman who desires a mate is to have a mate. Some men and women do not care to lead their Christian lives in the company of a spouse. Paul goes into detail about these specially gifted individuals in 1 Corinthians 7. However, because I assume my readers do not fall into this category, we can safely conclude that God's plan for you, if you so desire, is to be happily married. It is His will for your life.

God's will shall be done in your life, if you belong to Him and desire to live your life according to His Word. There are many confirmations of this truth in the Scriptures, and we'll cover them in detail as we go along, but for now, I want to direct your attention to an extraordinary promise contained in God's Word that pertains specifically to you. It is found in Isaiah 34:16: "Search from the book of the LORD, and read: Not one of these shall fail; not one shall lack her mate. For My mouth has commanded it, and His Spirit has gathered them."

Isn't that a great verse? You may not have noticed it before, and I'm putting it in the context of you and your own heart's desire, but there it is, shining forth in His Word; waiting for you to claim it. Go ahead and ask Him for your heart's desire, then relax in the knowledge that He shall do it. Relax and abide in the Lord. You won't be able to accomplish your goal, but the Lord will . . . He says so in His Word.

Remember that the "doing" shall be done by the Lord. It's particularly important to remember this if you are currently clinging to some guy in a life or death grip, trying desperately to get him to marry you. Let him go. It's more important that you pray. If he's yours, he'll stay. Meanwhile, you've got more important business to take care of. Your primary relationship must be with the Lord, for the Bible says He is our rock and our foundation. There is no substitute for talking to Him when it comes to building up our faith and our relationships. If your foundation with Christ is not strong, any human relationship you try to form will crumble. The bedrock of Christian marriage is Jesus. The hearts and souls of the man and woman must be knitted not only to each other, but jointly knitted to Him, so that they can build a strong relationship, a "threefold cord," that will be able to weather and endure the trials that will invariably come against them.

God calls you to be, now and always, a strong Christian first; and the only way to obtain the strength and stability you need in Him is to read the Word of God and pray. Your church can provide you with the instructions you need regarding your general prayer life. But, because this is a book on a specific issue, it's time to address the issue of prayer as it relates to our very special concern.

Chapter 2

The Importance of Prayer in the Dating/Mating Game

When I first became a Christian, I listened avidly to all the sermons and tapes I could find about prayer. It was such an exciting revelation to me that I could talk to God and that He would listen and answer. Jesus has a special way of dealing with the new Christian, of answering the smallest prayer in a manner that greatly builds your newfound faith. He responds the way a mother responds to the cries of her newborn baby.

I became like the kid with the new toy—every time God answered one of my little, almost unconscious prayers, I was thrilled with the knowledge that I was special to Him and that He loved me enough to take time to honor such an insignificant request. He always responded to me, sometimes immediately, but, invariably, I was given the answer before too much time had passed.

After a few years of toiling in the church, reading and studying the Bible, and living solely for the Lord, I was surprised to notice a renewed stirring in my heart for a mate. One night, in the quiet time of prayer, I was hit with the revelation that I didn't just "think it might be nice to be married." Rather, I realized that I *needed* to be married, that my truest and best destiny included loving and caring for, and being loved and cared for by a man, safely within the vows of marriage.

After this revelation I began to pray for a mate. The cry of my heart became, "Lord, hand him over." I fell on my knees nightly, fervently beseeching God. I cried and made promises; I bartered with and bombarded Jesus and sought His intercession with God Himself. I plunged into storming the gates of heaven with the single-minded intensity with which I tended to address most objectives in my life. Praying fervently, I kept one knee bowed and one eye open for the answer . . . for one month, two months, six months. Then I looked up and noticed that my position had not changed and neither had the Lord's. We were both exactly where we had been when I began to besiege Him.

No progress? But why not? Every little thing I had requested until this point had been met with instant gratification. Often, the whisper of a prayer was barely out of my lips before it was being answered. Why was I suddenly listening to the empty ring of unanswered prayer?

It is painful to confess my "spoiled brat" self, but she lives in me to this day and has to continually be reined in. Most all of my prayers, even those concerning a mate, were selfish ones . . ."Lord, do this for me; Lord, do that for me." Had I been aware, I would have heeded the exhortation: "You ask and do not receive, because you ask amiss, that you may spend it on your pleasures" (James 4:3).

I had always been shy and quiet, and nobody, before Jesus came into my life, had paid much attention to me; but like many shy people, I became even more self-centered. Although I was shy, I had always valued "me"; no matter what negative messages I received from others, my ego emerged intact. Though I was inhibited in my outward expression to the world, I didn't doubt that I was a special person. When the Lord found me, it only renewed my belief that He had created me for a special purpose.

The recognition that I was special in God's eyes was fine

and good, but praying for a mate involves much more than one's own precious self. There is now another person to consider. What is best for him? Is it you? What kind of wife and helpmate will you be? How will you be a blessing to him?

In the dark of night, on my knees, I learned to truly pray, and I learned about myself and my readiness to be a partner for life to a man whom God Himself had chosen. Were my prayers, motives, and desires selfish? God says such prayers will not be answered. That's because you are not the only person in the equation. Marriage does not represent instant gratification for one person. It is a blending of two of God's beloved. Believe it or not, He cares as much for the well-being of the man as He does for you, His precious female pearl. If you have not matured enough in the Lord to be willing to sacrifice, compromise, keep your temper, and follow the biblical injunction to submit to a husband, you probably are not yet ready to receive the answer to your prayer. It's not for nothing that you've heard the saying, "Be careful what you ask for because you might get it." Praying for a husband, which in actuality is praying to become a wife, is more than just an idle notion. For today's independent Christian woman, it indicates the willingness to change your attitudes and actions in areas in which you have long functioned alone. It is not always easy to relinquish that control, and we'll delve further into this reality in later chapters.

For now, pray and examine your heart, for the Lord will surely do so before He hands a man over to you.

WHAT TO PRAY FOR

Any discussion on praying for a mate invariably addresses the following questions: "What should I pray for?"; "How should I ask it?"; "Should I ask at all or just let Jesus answer the desires of my heart?" Surely there must be a thousand different questions and just as many answers.

During my time of "mating prayers," I tried every version I could think of. On some nights I presented a list to the

Lord—he has to look like this, be over six feet tall, weigh this much, work in this profession . . . on and on with my list of specific requirements. On other nights, I would adopt the posture of "Lord, give me the very best You have in store for me," then secretly hope that He knew what He was doing. Even my specific prayers changed from day to day. Understandably, when the Lord finally did begin to address my prayers in this regard, His responses to my requests were almost as varied as my prayers themselves.

One Friday night, on my way home from a business trip, I began to think about the husband of the saleswoman with whom I had been working. They had taken me out to dinner, and he seemed to be the handsomest, sweetest man I had ever met, who truly loved his wife. "Lord," I thought, "I'd like a husband just like him." This was not a real prayer, just a notion I expressed to God.

Two days later, on Sunday morning, I was seated in my customary seat in church, on a pew completely empty except for me and my children, when the exact double of my friend's husband walked in and sat twelve inches from my left side. He smiled, I smiled. My heart started pounding, buzzers went off in my head, and I immediately panicked. "Wait a minute, Lord. I know this is exactly who I asked for, but did You have to answer me so soon? I'm not sure I'm ready."

After smiling at each other during the service and sharing a brief chat afterwards, my "dream" man looked longingly at me, got into his car, and disappeared. All the way home, my kids kept asking, "Who was that man, Mom? I think he liked you." By then, all I wanted to do was cry over a lost opportunity. But when the Lord offers you an answer to a prayer and you decline, your only choice is to move on from there and realize that it really is *His* show, and not your choice that made the difference. My "dream guy" showed up and sat behind me about a month later. Although we again smiled, chatted, and tried to connect, by now I had solidified a whole new list of requirements, so it was easier to wave him good-bye and once again resume my posture of prayer for the right mate.

My advice to you, after having weathered several similar incidences, is to ask God for what you truly want, but only when you are *truly ready to receive it*. There is no way to gauge what I may have missed in those potential relationships, but because I was praying amiss, I was never really sure that any of those "misses" was truly God's answer to my prayer. There is no good reason to put yourself, another person, and God through the challenge of responding to your moods and whims. The Bible instructs us to pray without ceasing, but we must be sure to pray consistently without ceasing. The Lord says of a waffler, "He is a double-minded man, unstable in all his ways" (James 1:8), and so, too, is a double-minded woman. On the other hand, God may simply be waiting until you have made up your mind, while you continue praying hither and yon, wondering all the while hy He's not answering you.

I personally don't feel that your best choice is to pray for specific attributes unless they are all you are willing to accept; for the Lord will indeed answer your specific prayer, but it may not be the very *best* He had intended for you. Recently, a newly married male friend of mine was lamenting that if he ever married again, if there was ever going to be a next time, he would pray differently. His request had been, "God, let her be spiritual." His new wife is the most spiritual woman I have ever met, always on her knees before the Lord and seeking after lost souls, but he says, "It's the little foxes that destroy the vine." Now, he would also pray that she clean up the hair she leaves all over the bathroom and pick up around the house once in a while. For her part, she says she would no longer pray, "Lord, let him be a preacher." She would also add, "Lord, give him a steady income." So, stop trying to dictate to God what you need—you don't really know.

Take time to truly search your own heart instead. Spend time with Jesus, not in beseeching "mating prayers," but asking Him for direction and guidance. Let Him know that the deepest desire of your heart is to receive the husband He has for you and be sure that is really the truth. Ask Him to make you ready to receive the man He has for you. It is fine to have a list of physical attributes in mind, but don't hold yourself or God bound until He delivers to your exact specifications. Keep your heart open and your spirit in tune with Christ. He may choose to open up possibilities for you in ways you have not yet considered. It is foolish to tie God's hands. He knows you; therefore, He knows what type of man is best for you. You will be delightfully surprised at how well He has chosen.

THE READINESS FACTOR

We will be dealing with the "readiness" issue in one form or another throughout this book, but here, while we are specifically discussing prayer, it is vital to note that you must ask God to prepare your heart to receive what He has to offer. In so doing, expect to confront yourself in ways you have not yet done, in areas that will open up a new awareness of yourself. You will find that the openness of your heart and submission of your will to His are the essential concessions that you must make as He prepares you to become a Christian wife. If you are like me, your very fiber rebels against the word and the notion of "submission," but it is the key to a happy and peaceful life, both as a Christian and as a wife.

We are, in fact, talking about relinquishing control, no longer being the sole "master of your fate." However, we are not talking about becoming a slave, a robot, or a possession. God gave you your distinct personality for His own reasons. It is a surety that He will also give you a mate who complements and responds to the uniqueness that He created in you. Submission to a husband is not a "yield, heel, bow down" proposition. Rather, it is the willingness to allow another person to assume a role of responsibility for you. There will be numerous areas of discussion and compromise in your marriage, but there can be only one head. God, in His Word, says that the responsibility of headship is given to the man.

Focus on maintaining your openness to the instruction that God is giving you. Remember, you can't fool God. He truly does know when you are ready for a mate because He will see to it that you become comfortable with the notion of obeying Him first. It is not His desire to oppress you or to stifle your rights as a human being. In fact, wholehearted submission to God will free you to calm down and enjoy your life in ways you never thought possible.

Chapter 3

Just Say No

Let's set the record straight on another essential ingredient in your preparation to receive the husband you have been praying for. You have committed your heart to God and are learning to submit your will to His Word. It's now time to take another look at that Word, and to closely examine one of the primary rules it contains for the single Christian.

- 1 Corinthians 6:18. "Flee sexual immorality. Every sin that a man does is outside the body, but he who commits sexual immorality sins against his own body."
- 1 Corinthians 6:13. "Now the body is not for sexual immorality but for the Lord, and the Lord for the body."
- 1 Thessalonians 4:3. "For this is the will of God, your sanctification: that you should abstain from sexual immorality."
- 1 Thessalonians 4:4. "That each of you should know how to possess his own vessel in sanctification and honor."
- Romans 6:12. "Therefore do not let sin reign in your mortal body, that you should obey it in its lusts."

There are forty other passages in the Bible that rank sexual sins as being detestable in God's sight. Some verses you might want to review include Proverbs 6:32, Ezekiel 16:15, Matthew 15:19, Acts 15:29, 1 Corinthians 10:8, Jude 7, and

Revelation 2:20. I could list many more, but they can all be found in a concordance. Look them up.

In this age of AIDS and other sexually transmitted diseases, "safe sex" seems to be a ubiquitous warning. However, the biblical injunction gets lost and, by the way in which the world presents the warning, mocked. God's standard is much higher than that implied in the dictionary definition of fornication as "voluntary sexual intercourse between an unmarried woman and a man." You, of course, already know that, just as you already know that it is a sin. It is what you choose to do with this knowledge that is one of the most vital issues you will confront. "Safe sex" is not the concern. Your relationship with God and with your future husband is. The Bible says that you must abstain from sex outside the vows of marriage. There is no way around it. There is never justification for having sex with a man to whom you are not married.

Now let's break this down further. Put your instincts aside and don't get defensive. We are here to listen to and learn from God. Keep in mind the goal of openness to His will that you've been seeking to build in your heart. If this strikes a nerve, say "Ouch," and continue to listen and learn, and put into practice what God says you should do. Let's try phrasing it another way. You shall not have sex with a man unless he is your husband. Having sexual desire is not a sufficient reason, and the fact that you may have long since lost your virginity is irrelevant. Fornication is a *voluntary* act. You, therefore, have the ability to say no. It is your choice to make. And you must say no, regardless of who the man is, Christian or not (and Christian men don't always say no to sex). As a Christian woman you must say it and mean it.

VALUE YOURSELF OR HE WON'T

Most Christians have to struggle with sexual desires. It is part of human nature to enjoy sex; consequently, it is one of the biggest issues of self-control that most people confront. The attraction of the opposite sex and the temptations of

Satan to indulge in sexual relations have proven to be a weakness for all too many Christians, married or single. No, if you engage in sexual relations outside of marriage you do not lose your salvation; this is a sin that God forgives, even though Matthew 5:32 and 19:9 show that God considers sexual immorality in the form of adultery to be a sin sufficiently vile to justify divorce, which He hates. But for you, as a Christian woman, the consequences are far greater. You are the "pearl of great price," "the gem of great value." First Corinthians 6:18 states that when you participate in sex outside of marriage, you are sinning against yourself, your body, and your testimony as a Christian. You harm yourself; you are the victim of your own action.

It is not a "safe sex" issue. If you don't value yourself as a special woman, you can bet that neither will a man. It is a fact of human nature that we seldom esteem something we can get for free. Anything being given away automatically loses most of its perceived worth. If you don't prize your body and view it as a precious gift to be sought after and treasured, no man will. And once it's been given away, you can never get it back from him. The Lord will forgive you for your "slipup," but the man seldom does. He'll be off instead, once again, on his quest to find a "good" woman.

Most women, even very jaded ones, are shocked by the "provincial" values of most men. Even the most morally permissive man views a woman who has equally permissive attitudes as being morally lax. Men, invariably, divide women into categories of "good girls" and "bad girls" . . . those who are "easy" and those who are not. It doesn't do a bit of good to rail against the injustice of the judgment—it still exists in the male mind. Whether they were raised that way or not, men exhibit a marked decrease in respect for women with whom they can easily engage in sex, while some women still believe that being a "one-night stand" can lead to marriage.

You, God's precious pearl, must be the one to say "no."

You cannot depend upon someone else to be moral for you or to be responsible for your actions. No matter what the man's urgings and suggestions may be, God commands that you show respect for yourself. You'll find that far from chasing a man away, your "no" will greatly increase his respect for you and his overall estimation of your worth.

SATAN IS A LIAR—YOU CAN WAIT

As time passed during my "mating prayers" season, I became increasingly anxious to meet a man. My situation seemed pretty bleak; no matter how hard I tried, there were no marriage candidates around, but there were plentiful opportunities for casual sex. Conventional advice counsels single women to do whatever it takes to get a man, but God says He has what it takes. I decided to stop searching and to listen to God instead. When I took my hands off what I viewed as my dire mating situation and decided to stop chasing men down, I suddenly found that my opportunities for sex dried up and disappeared. After becoming a Christian, I had permitted myself to engage in sex on an extremely sporadic basis, usually when I was out of town on a business trip. For some reason, I figured the Lord had not followed me to the new city, and I was on some kind of vacation from my convictions. Whenever I found a man, or rather, when some man went through extraordinary efforts to land me in bed on one of those trips, I thanked God for His "gift," enjoyed the moment, and thought nothing of it afterward.

Then one Sunday morning, my pastor preached a scathing message on fornication, and my eyes were opened wide enough to see what the Lord was saying to me. I was still a "baby" Christian. As yet, I had been under no condemnation about sex. I felt it was only "human nature" to engage in occasional sex. Suddenly, it was brought to my attention and birthed in my spirit that this was, in fact, a grievous sin, one that had direct consequences on my relationship with Jesus Christ. I immediately came under God's conviction, for I realized that He was talking to *me*; and I could not deny that I understood the message.

I prayed for forgiveness, asked for His strength, and instantly ceased all participation in sex. My sexual activity and interest in sex vanished to the point where celibacy was no longer an issue, and participation in sex was not even a passing inclination. God completely removed the desire from me, and I consciously removed myself from any situations where temptations might arise. I became committed to living my life as God would have me live it, rather than attracting a man. In the past, I had hoped to turn guys on; now, I only wanted to turn to the Lord.

When you take a position of total commitment to God, He honors it. For the three years from that point until I married, I abstained from all sexual contact, while still praying my "mating prayers." I was free to talk to men, to form friendships with them, to date and enjoy their company, but there was no sex involved, or anything remotely resembling sex. And three years is not such a long time. Some of the happily married Christian women I know, whose stories will be shared later in this book, abstained from sex for many years. They did so by the grace of God, and with His blessing and assistance. In every case, both they and their husbands have vivid testimonies of the Lord helping them to abstain from sex. He can and will do the same for you, if you so desire. No matter what Satan whispers in your ear, sexual immorality does not have to be a part of your relationship with a man. But you have to make the commitment to wait until God blesses your marriage union.

GOD BADE ME DO IT

The Bible states in Proverbs 12:4, that "An excellent wife is the crown of her husband, but she who causes shame is like rottenness in his bones." I still derive a great deal of pleasure from listening to my husband telling others about our courtship. He attests, without hesitation, to the respect he gained for me as a woman and the ways in which he grew as a man and as a Christian, during the early stages of our relationship. When we first met, I had been celibate for over two years, but he was a recently born-again Christian. After a lifetime of attending church, he had finally been saved, and although he deeply loved the Lord, his relationship with Christ had not yet grown to the point where it impinged in any way upon his lifestyle. Like most other males that I had encountered, he was incredulous over the fact that I would have nothing to do with fornication.

Even though he was a "saved" man, unbeknownst to me, he had long maintained a steady relationship with a Christian woman who felt that casual sex was not a problem. She viewed it as leading to marriage; he saw it as easy sex. When he and I met, his opinion was that sex was a readily forgiven sin in which he, as a Christian, could indulge with minimum consequences.

At first, he viewed my unwillingness to participate in "lovemaking" as an intriguing challenge . . . surely I couldn't resist him. He mildly invited it and waited to see what would happen . . . nothing. He attempted a few passionate goodnight kisses . . . nothing. Grabbing and caressing earned him only rebuke and an early ejection from my house. Much later, he boasted about the fact that I had never let him see the inside of my bedroom, even though he made it an issue while we were dating. Today he says that marriage was not on his mind at all when we first began dating but that he became increasingly fascinated by the vow I had made with God, by the seriousness of my relationship with Christ, and by my commitment to honoring God's work in my body. We began to have frequent discussions concerning his inability to believe that a person could actually live without sex. In his opinion, the Bible's prohibitions against premarital sex and its descriptions of a "virtuous" woman were only an unattainable ideal. He never felt he could meet God's standards so neither could anyone else. But Proverbs 14:12 states, "There is a way that seems right to a man, but its end is the way of death." When he finally began to listen, to understand, and to believe, his walk with Christ changed and grew. God got his attention and began to work in his life in a very real way.

I later learned that after several months of courtship, and finally engagement, his sexual partner asked him if he was sleeping with me. To his great surprise, upon hearing "No," she became enraged. Perhaps she had a right to be . . . she felt he had disrespected her worth both as a Christian and as a woman. From his point of view, however, he owed her nothing. He was sleeping only with her and her response to his advances had been completely voluntary. Since she had willingly participated, and had, presumably, accepted as readily as he had the fact of their sexual sin, he felt that her "Yes" to his request in no way obligated him. From the beginning, he had been honest about not wanting to marry her, so when he met me, he assumed he now had a great situation going . . . one Christian woman whose companionship he enjoyed, and another Christian woman with whom he could enjoy a guilt-free sexual relationship. However, for obvious reasons, God couldn't allow such a delicate balancing of women to continue in his life. When he decided to marry me, he told her of his decision, and inadvertently said good-bye to sexual activity until our wedding night.

At no point did I ever use my convictions as a conscious show or demonstration to anyone. Rather, I just let the Lord direct my actions. Your situation is probably very different. He may require that you put an end to the sexual part of a relationship you are already in. Maybe He'll tell you to stop sleeping with, or even living with, a guy with whom you have been involved for years. He can free you from the notion that sex is essential to maintaining your relationship with a man. You will find that it is not. Your friendship with each other and your ability to communicate and understand and like each other are far more important. Many a woman has feared that when she began to value herself and her body and stopped giving herself away for free her man would cease to love her. In reality, your abstinence will work far more to your benefit than you ever imagined, for sex always clouds a relationship. Its absence will clearly bring into focus your true feelings for each other, the ones that don't involve lust. As I have stated earlier, if he is, in fact, your man, he will stay around. Furthermore, he might even decide to marry you. In any case, if he is a Christian, he will immediately understand your position, and if he is not, you have much praying to do; first of all for his salvation . . . sex is the least of your worries. If he is not a Christian, he won't understand much of anything about you.

If, despite your best intentions, you find yourself in a situation that threatens to turn into sexual activity, there is one very effective technique that will bring you to your senses immediately. You know, spiritually and intellectually, that Jesus is in you; take Him out of the intangible and put Him in the flesh, sitting right there next to you on the bed, or the sofa, or wherever, silently watching your every move. The resulting check on your passions should see you safely out of the danger of the moment. God truly is with you at all times. He loves you and only plans the best for you; and if you obey Him, that's exactly what you'll receive.

CELIBACY—NOT A TREND BUT A COMMITMENT

Satan will tell you that sex is only natural; that you need it for your health and psychological well-being; that you can only go for so long before you've got to have it. He'll tell you that you really can't say no and mean it.

God tells you, instead, that sex is not necessary for your body, and that fornication brings death and destruction to your relationships and quite possibly to your mental and physical health; and that you can and must be celibate before you marry. It is not an option for the Christian . . . God demands it.

The world is now busily touting the "C" word as if celibacy is a last resort, an extraordinary measure to be taken as a means of combating disease and death. Society views celibacy as an aberration from the norm, feeling that once we get all this sickness and disease under control, we can return to the hard-earned sexual rights we have won in the past. It is not going to happen. Satan is a liar and the truth is not in him. God's Word and His laws will not be thwarted. Society, as much as it may wish for it, will never return to the days of easy sex and "free love," because God has not ordained it.

You, a single Christian woman, can avoid Satan's sexual trap if you pray and commit yourself to following His Word. No matter how long you've been sexually active, you must stop now. Knowledge is a powerful thing, for when you know an action is wrong and you continue to participate, for you, it is even more sinful. Second Peter 2:21 states, "For it would have been better for them not to have known the way of righteousness, than having known it, to turn from the holy commandment delivered to them." Now you know . . . God's will for you is to avoid fornication. Your clean body and mind are the temple of the Holy Spirit and the gift from God to you, and to the future mate you are preparing to receive.

Yes, you can say no. You will respect yourself, and your husband-to-be will respect and value you even more than you value yourself. The dividends you will reap by delaying sex until you have married are more to be desired than the degradation and guilt you will face by willfully ignoring God's Word. Don't let Satan take control of your mind and your temple. He is indeed a liar, and you can prove him so by the grace of God working in you.

Chapter 4

How Not to Do It

You've been praying. You've made the desires of your heart perfectly clear to God. You are refraining from sexual activity, and have asked for His help in every other area of your life as well. And you know in your very soul that the answer to your prayer is imminent. So you decide to help God along. "Well," you reason, "my mate is not just going to come up and knock on the front door. I should be doing something." I'm not going to tell you that this urge is wrong. In fact, I believe that it is a nudge coming straight from the Lord Himself. You did not commit your life to be a hermit, nor did God call you to hide away in a convent. You can enjoy your life and find pleasure in it with God's blessings. And, no, a husband most likely will not come up and knock on your door. You've got to be "about your Father's business," living your life and interacting with the people in it. You'll be a happier, more well-adjusted person for doing so. The surest path for not realizing God's plan for your life is to sit alone in your living room, waiting for Him to spring it into action without any effort on your part. That won't happen in any area of your life.

"SO WHAT CAN I BE DOING?"

CALL OFF THE MATE SEARCH

I have always been a willful woman, with a profound appreciation for my own initiative. When I was in the world, I ran my own life in my own way, without benefit of mother or father or anyone else's unwanted opinion. And when I became a Christian, I was still bent on running the show myself. When the mating urge struck me full force, I saw no reason to control my inclination to help God out. "Okay, God," I thought, "just show me where to go and what to do, and I'll take care of the rest." Because all of my previous man-hunting experience had taken place in the worldly arena, I went back to the old haunts as a stalking ground. Very bad move. It's hard enough to find any man in the nightclub, party, and bar scene; it is impossible to unearth a Christian man there. Oh, I talked to a lot of guys and ended up stunning them and scaring them off when I announced that Jesus Christ was the Lord of my life. Besides, I now felt very strange and out of place sitting in a smoky club filled with drinkers, listening to music I no longer enjoyed, suppressing the urge to go up and preach to the people around me. That's not God's way to meet people—it's the world's, and as a Christian, it just won't work for you.

Remember, you must not set out to find a mate. That is the worst possible thing to waste time and energy on. Every man is not "maybe the right one." Turning over every rock on the beach rarely leads to the discovery of anything precious. Remember who the pearl is. The search is not yours to make.

When I finally realized the futility of trying to extract God's best from the dross of the world's worst, I threw up my hands in defeat, which was exactly what I needed to do all along. Out of pure frustration, I took my hands off the situation, stopped trying to control it, and let God begin to work it out His way. I can just hear the Lord saying, "Great. It's about time."

I didn't stop going to work, or meeting friends for lunch, or going to basketball games or picnics. And every time the church door opened, I was there—Sunday morning, Sunday night, Tuesday women's studies, Wednesday Bible study. I went to anything and everything that interested me. The difference was that I no longer had one eye open for a mate.

I stopped measuring every man for his potential as my husband and I ceased to anticipate that the perfect guy was always just around the next corner. In fact, I released my hands from the situation to such an extent that I even released God from any promise that I would marry at all. I quit praying "mating prayers" because I was certain that God now knew that I was ready to marry. The answer was up to Him.

One night during prayer time, I announced to the Lord that if He wanted me to have a mate, He'd have to bring him and sit him down next to me in church because that would be the only place I would be found. As far as I was concerned, the search was over, and the most important thing in my life was to develop an intimate relationship with Christ. I meant it—getting to know Jesus had suddenly become my consuming concern.

It truly is amazing what God will do when you hand yourself and your problem over to Him. Not long after I made my pronouncement, the incident I related earlier occurred—an interested man appeared and sat by my side in church, but it was as yet too early for me to know how to properly respond. I had not become comfortable enough with the Lord's answers to my prayers to trust and react to them immediately, but this man did let me know that God was listening.

Several months later the man I would marry also showed up and sat next to me in church. This time, I was ready.

Once the Lord assumes total control over your life, you'll find that you actually can trust your instincts and your feelings, for they have been reordered to operate in a Christian mode.

The biggest risk you will run is getting impatient and acting on impulse. It takes time, but you must learn to recognize the voice of God, and to know when He is leading you and when He is not. If the urge feels wrong; if the response is the same one you would have made before you Became a Christian, then it is wrong and is not from God. Thinking that you have to compromise your principles to find a man is wrong. Joining your non-Christian friends or coworkers to go on a manhunt is wrong. Feeling that you have to dress and act sexy to attract a man is wrong. Readopting your previous flirting techniques is wrong. None of these will accomplish your goal. It's time to shut up that nagging little voice from your old self, the one who thinks that the only ways that work are the old ways, the dross you should have discarded and left far behind by now. Besides, those ways were the ones that worked with wordly men; they won't do any good at all with the Christian you now seek.

YOU CAN'T JUDGE A MAN BY HIS COVER

You must let go of your old criteria and arbitrary standards for evaluating a man. The Bible states:

- John 7:24. "Do not judge according to appearance, but judge with righteous judgment."
- 1 Samuel 16:7. "Do not look at his appearance or at his physical stature. . . . For the LORD does not see as man sees; for man looks at the outward appearance, but the LORD looks at the heart."
- 2 Corinthians 10:7. "Do you look at things according to the outward appearance?"

The point that the Bible is making is that the surface gives you no true indication of the whole. It tells you no more than the appearance of a calm sea, underneath which are currents that run deep and strong. Your priority now must be to recognize and appreciate the heart of a man as much or more than you do the fact that he is handsome, or well-built, or financially secure. The day is going to come when his face will change, his hair will thin, his body will get a bit heftier, and the riches will either fade away or won't buy nearly as much. When the inevitable happens to the outside, you will still be left with, hopefully, loving the man himself.

Of course, we know that there are certain men you are attracted to, based solely on appearance. They are your type. God will operate within that framework of personal attraction. It is not necessary that you settle for a short, round, bald Christian, when you would prefer a taller, thinner Christian, with a full head of hair. But, on the other hand, if He brings a friendly, short, round, and bald man into your life, don't be afraid to get to know him. There are many possible reasons why he is there, and if you don't desire marriage to him, that obviously is not the reason he's there in the first place. He may have come into your life to teach you something, or perhaps you should introduce him to one of your single friends, or he may have a friend or relative you need to meet. He may even have come into your life for you to minister to him. Just keep the possibilities open whenever you meet a nice Christian, male or female. Think beyond yourself and your quest for marriage. There needs to be a place in your life for friendships to develop, as well.

Now, let's get to the heart of the matter. The single most important criterion for the man you marry is that he be a *believer in Christ*, not just a member of a church. If you are a Christian, you already understand what that means. A man's membership in church is always a good start, but it is not enough; his relationship with Christ must be genuine. You may have noticed that throughout this book, I have been referring to Christian men in the context of your husband-to-be. That is because it is a requirement of God. When we read in 2 Corinthians 6:14, "Do not be unequally yoked together with unbelievers," the passage is referring to the context of marriage, as well as business partnerships and other ventures. Without this equality of faith, your marriage cannot have a strong foundation on which to be built. There will be too many battles to be fought in other areas of your life; it is ridiculous to subject yourself and your primary relationship in life to stress in this fundamental area of belief. No, he doesn't have to be a spiritual giant, but he must care enough about God to pray, read his Bible, and try to serve Christ to the best of his abilities, as you seek to do.

And, since we usually marry one of the people we have

dated, it is probably wise to date only Christians. There are differing views on this within the Christian community. Some hold that you should associate yourself only with other Christians, while others feel that dating unbelievers is acceptable on a level of friendship. They feel that the Lord has the final say, and that it is possible that your friendship with the unbelieving man can lead to his salvation. There are married Christian couples who will readily attest that such was the case in their relationship.

I feel that your best and only choice is to pray about the matter. If you feel strongly that you should limit your dating to Christians, that's great. If you do decide to venture into the non-Christian arena, you must do so cautiously and prayerfully, particularly if you are still a new Christian or a babe in Christ. Non-Christians are not the enemy. They are people—nice, intelligent, attractive, kind, and interesting, just the way you were before you came to know Christ. But, the fact that you belong to Christ means there is now a crucial difference between you and them. They are not the same as you anymore. It is a common trick of the devil to use your desires and naivete to lull you into falsely believing that the man you find so appealing, usually for surface reasons, can be converted. That is rarely the case. The reality is that the more time a baby Christian spends with an unbelieving man, the easier it becomes for her to backslide. The pleas of the man for sex, his denial of her Christian experience, his logic, or open hostility to God, can often wear down her resistance, and put her relationship with Jesus Christ through an unproductive test. The result, whether she gives in or stands strong, is usually a broken relationship, and/or a broken heart. It is seldom worth it.

If you have been a Christian for quite awhile, and feel the urge to date an attractive unbeliever, pray and seriously examine your motives. You may find, somewhere in the back of your mind, that another snare from Satan is lurking. Have you decided, consciously or unconsciously, that you are tired of waiting, that this man looks good to you, and that God will forgive you anyway? Have you decided that money or prestige really are important to you, and that in order to obtain them, you can live with his unbelief? You may find, to your surprise, that God lets you proceed with your plans, and that you set yourself up for endless rounds of prayer and grief in the future. It is a very painful thing to know that the man you love is headed straight for hell. It is just as bad to have to fight heavy resistance or endure cold indifference when you pray, read your Bible, or attend church. You may find that willful disobedience to God extracts a fearsome toll, both on your peace of mind and on your marriage. And who knows what marital blessings God may have planned for you had you waited.

All told, your chance of going out, getting a man, and bringing him into the fold is extremely poor. The path of marriage outside of Christ is rocky, and subject to all of the storms that Satan can bring against it. These are serious considerations you must make before allowing the world and its lures to decide your affairs of the heart. Whose criteria do you choose? You can do no better than to follow the example of Joshua, who said, "As for me and my house, we will serve the LORD" (Josh. 24:15).

DON'T SAY "GOD SAYS IT'S YOU"

Most Christians, fortunately, prefer to spend time in church or in Bible study; they prefer the company of other Christians and find, with them, camaraderie of the Spirit. They draw strength from each other, and their faith is renewed whenever they feel weak and tempted to give up. God designed it that way. You will be happiest, and enjoy your life as God intended it, in the company of other believers.

However, for the single Christian woman, this frequently leads to a problem of a different sort. You, along with a billion or so of your sisters, have restricted your activities to church, you date only Christian men, and now you find yourself limited to a setting that is predominantly female, where an unattached Christian male is a cause for celebration. He is

usually pleasantly surprised to find that, whether good-looking or not, he is surrounded by dozens of attractive, well-
dressed, friendly women, all of whom are wondering, "Is this
one going to be my husband?" Subtle and not-so-subtle bids
will be made for his attention, sometimes even by parents in
the church who are scouting for their single daughters. He
usually becomes busy and happy, and not too eager to make
a final decision on a wife.

Phase 1—The Prophecy/Prediction Syndrome

This unfortunate shortage of single Christian men leads
many women, particularly in more charismatic churches, to
fall victim to what I call the Prophecy/Prediction Syndrome.
In the small, nondenominational church I attended for a
while, where the gifts of prophecy and tongues were fully
evident, the Syndrome was quite common. A typical scenario
is created by a woman whose mating urge is in full bloom.
She has been praying and beseeching the Lord for months,
or maybe years. Suddenly a new man arrives at church, or
perhaps he is already in place at a new church she has joined.
In any case, he looks like the man she has been waiting for.
Whether or not he shares her attraction is irrevelant. At first
she tries to maintain control and to not be too obvious around
him, to wait on God, but she finds her prayers are taking on
a new direction. He begins to show up in them sometimes,
and maybe in her dreams, as well.

She decides to become a bit friendlier to him. Maybe she
seeks him out for special Christian hugs, or always has a smile
or a helpful word for him. Sometimes he develops a mild
though not serious interest, or he may remain totally unaf-
fected. She is undeterred from what is becoming increasingly
obvious to her. She starts to ask the Lord about him, then
begins to tell the Lord about him. Her prayers change from
"Lord, is he the one?" to "Lord, he is the one." If the relationship, either real or potential, seems to not be developing swiftly
enough, or not along the lines she wants, a hint of doubt enters
the picture. She is, after all, a saved woman . . . she must look

to the Lord for her answers. During prayer time she once again questions, "Lord, is he the one?" The subtext to the question is actually "Lord, show me a sign that he is the one."

And, in the context of the female heart, that sign could be just about anything. Maybe it's a shy smile from him or a vivid dream in which he stars. Whatever it is, something occurs that confirms her fondest hope. She now feels that God has spoken to her.... Yes, he is indeed the one she is destined to marry. She is joyful and excited, and full of anticipation. Time passes, however, and nothing seems to be changing between them. She then enters into a period of intense prayer, from which she emerges with the conviction that it's finally time to share God's exciting revelation with the man.

One way or another, she finds a way to talk to him alone, and announces the fateful news, "God has shown me that you are going to be my husband." Filled with a combination of joy and apprehension, she finds herself confronting a dismayed man whose urge is not to sweep her into his arms, as she would have preferred, but to run as fast as he can. He usually proceeds to promptly disengage her from his life.

The scenario just described normally unfolds over a period of months. It takes time to work up a fully developed belief that you have actually heard from the very mouth of God, when in reality, you have heard yourself putting words into God's mouth.

"Well," you might be asking, "what's wrong with what she did? Who are you to say she didn't hear from God? How do you know that?"

I know, because as arbitrary as my evaluation may seem, it is actually based on the Word of God.

What Went Wrong?

Let's consider the errors our friend made in her assumptions and actions. They could not have occurred had she truly listened to God, and not acted from her own emotional desires.

Not every word you receive from God is meant to be shared. Most of God's words to you are for your edification alone, and should be kept between you and God. David, in

Psalm 141:3 prays, "Set a guard, O LORD, over my mouth; keep watch over the door of my lips." Proverbs 29:11 says, "A fool vents all his feelings, but a wise man holds them back." Sharing an intimate revelation of this sort is almost always a major mistake. All men, Christians included, prefer to make their own choice of a woman. They like to think it's their decision, even when it's been the woman's goal all along. The man's need to feel he is the decision maker, the leader, is part of his nature. We'll discuss this in more detail in chapter 14. By verbalizing her prophecy, our friend has taken away his option—he seems himself to be a pawn in a plan concocted between her and God; and he will almost always automatically reject it because his input in the matter seems to have been disregarded.

God will not tell one person without telling the other. Just as He revealed His plan to her, He will also open the man's eyes to the revelation. It is not her place to try to open up his eyes. God will notify the man Himself, since the wills of both people are involved. If the prophecy was truly from God, it would not take the guy totally by surprise. He would already have received at least some indication that marriage to this woman was possibly in God's plan for him. And she would have felt no need to prod him into action by making her announcement. God will not manipulate a man and his desires to suit another person's will. The man's own choice is a critical factor.

She stepped outside His will when she decided to stop waiting. Whenever you receive a message from God, the Bible says you must wait for Him to bring it to pass, in order to know that it is truly from Him. First John 4:1 instructs us, "Do not believe every spirit, but test the spirits, whether they are of God; because many false prophets have gone out into the world." Acting on your own, in an attempt to speed God up, can short-circuit God's plan, making it null and void. When you try to take it away from God and run with it yourself, you have already blown it.

Her apprehension alone should have served as sufficient warning that all was not right with the action she was considering. God never lets you just blunder ahead without warning you and trying to prevent you from acting rashly and getting hurt. She forged ahead on the erroneous mental assumption that the man's response would automatically be positive, even though her intuition (God's spiritual prompting) told her it would not be so. She felt that if she verbally expressed the thought, it could become reality. In fact, she was practicing a form of magical thinking, which holds that you can speak a thing into existence. Although it is loosely based on the fact that God spoke and all things were created, in most instances, it is an attempt to manipulate God and a situation by wishful thinking. It is a belief commonly held not only by Christians, but by all sorts of people, including New Age philosophers. It doesn't work. You may speak forth all you want, but unless God *wills* a thing to be, *nothing* will happen. Speaking out your revelation will never prompt God into action, or a man into marriage.

Phase 2—Post-Revelation Anxiety

There is a Phase 2 of the Prophecy/Prediction Syndrome. After erroneously sharing her revelation with her intended, and watching in dismay as he heads in the opposite direction, many a woman takes a stand, defiantly waiting for the man's attitude to change. She spends time trying to chase off other women by announcing to anyone who will listen that he is her man—God told her so. She telephones sweetly, tries to stay on her nicest behavior, and watches vigilantly for any sign of a shift in his position. She has heard from the Lord; this man is not going to change that fact. She is fully prepared to wait him out. By now, she has decided that it might take years, yet, despite all discouragement, she will hold fast.

She now begins to pray on him. These are very special, devoutly intense prayers intended to remind God of what He has said. They are usually along the lines of "God, You said he's to be my husband. Lord, I'm holding You to Your promise.... Make it come to pass." I have several male friends who are in the throes of being prayed on by women they have no intention of ever marrying.

I also have several female friends who are thoroughly and resolutely convinced that God has shown them their husbands, but the guys just don't know it yet. Most of these women have already notified their intended husbands and are waiting with varying degrees of impatience for the "revelation" to take hold in the men. One of my male friends, however, had no idea what was going on when the women in his small church began scowling and looking at him strangely. Finally an older sister chastized him about how badly he was treating a woman he barely knew. That's when he discovered that instead of telling him about her marriage revelation, the woman had shared the news with her entire women's study group, and they were all concerned about his seeming indifference. As is typical, my male friend has no intention of ever marrying this particular woman, although she has been waiting for several years.

LET GO OF THE DEATH GRIP

It's the only way to get on with your life. If God has given you a revelation about a specific man as your husband-to-be, first of all, calm down. Then relax and let him go. Release the man from your mating prayers and from any expectations about how it will all work out. You can't presume to hold God to a plan of action; for here, as is the case with most of His responses to prayers, the answer is likely to come in a way you least expect. You cannot anticipate God's moves, for they rarely, if ever, follow the paths you have laid out for them. He is the Sovereign God. You are not in control. He is.

A word is appropriate here about the Prediction portion of the Syndrome. You need to stop, be still, and try to ascertain what it is you have actually received. A prediction is a revelation made without input from God. It is a human judgment, based on human thought and rationale. The difference between the two becomes apparent only when God steps in to prove that the revelation is true. If the event you feel has been foretold to you never comes to pass, what you have made is a prediction. Only time can confirm the truth.

You must be extremely careful not to put your entire life on indefinite hold, while you focus on waiting for God to finish up this husband business. If the revelation is genuine, and not based on your fears, lusts, or emotions, then its reality will be proven without any prompting from you. You will know in your spirit, beyond a shadow of doubt, that what has been revealed to you will come to pass. Instead of causing you to become frantic, His word to you should bring joy and the "peace of God, which surpasses all understanding" (Phil. 4:7). You'll find that sitting back and watching God work is far more exciting, and a far better builder of your faith, than jumping ahead of Him and trying to do it yourself. Resting in it is the only way to prove what God has said.

God's revelation to you may be true, but as we have seen, uttering it aloud is a very dangerous move, for that action immediately casts you into the role of prophet. Others are now watching and waiting to see if what you have declared actually comes to pass. Because so many husband-to-be prophecies have proven untrue, they are often characterized as "prophe-lying," instead of prophesying; that is, declaring a thing yourself and accusing God of saying or ordaining it. Learn to try the voices you hear, for 1 John 4:1 directs us to "test the spirits, whether they are of God." Learn to discern between the whispers of your flesh, the promptings from Satan, and the direct revelation of God. If you do receive a revelation of this nature, be content with "knowing in your knower," and leave the prophesying alone.

Letting go of the death grip means letting go of your will, as much as it means letting go of the man. No matter how difficult it may be, your best response toward your intended is to be quiet, stay sweet and friendly, and nonaggressive. Almost any move you make toward prompting the man into action will backfire. Don't cut yourself off from other men and other friends. Though it will not be easy, stop focusing on him as your mate-to-be. Pray about it and ask the Lord to allow him to recede into the back of your mind, so that he does not become an obsession with you. No one appreciates being stalked by another person who has the persistence of a heat-seeking missile. All your worrying, obsessing, and scheming will not accomplish God's plan one bit faster. The Bible says that "not My will, but Yours, be done" (Luke 22:42). This is the attitude we must take. If you cannot stay focused on God rather than on a man, you will only succeed in making your life miserable. Of course, you are free to treat him as your friend, and to enjoy his company, if he wants to be with you; but you must not attempt to push further than that. Don't panic if he doesn't suddenly decide he's in love with you. With some men, the revelation that they want a specific woman as their wife comes instantly; with many others, the attraction develops over time. And if no attraction exists at all, none of your proddings or attempts at seduction will work. If this is the case, if "your" man shows no desire for you at all, if you are definitely not his type, it is unlikely that God has ordained him to be your husband. Your "revelation" about him exists primarily in your mind. True, all things are possible with God, and perhaps God will change his mind, but your actions won't. You must calm down and let go of your expectation of him. Don't even expect God to work it out.

There is no other way around it—if God has said, "It's you," sit back, hold your peace, and wait. It's *His* plan that's going to be put into action, not yours.

Chapter 5

Understanding God's Timetable

You are probably thinking by now, "I'm ready. Why do you keep talking about waiting? I've been waiting. I don't even have a man on the horizon. What can I do about *that*?" Well, you're not really as ready as you think. You must still learn to live peaceably with God's schedule. Back in chapter 2, we talked about readiness. Everything we have discussed to this point hinges solely upon God's decision to bring it to pass. Your mating prayers, your waiting, and your preparation to receive are all preliminary steps to ready yourself for God's answer to your prayer. Even though you're standing at the starting line, bright and shiny and ready to go, it is entirely possible that nothing will happen yet. The pistol still won't sound.

Why? Here's something to consider—you are not the one who decides on your readiness. God may need to test and try, to hone and sharpen, and to strengthen your faith first. First Peter 5:10 states that God wants to "perfect, establish, strengthen, and settle you." He wants you to get to know Him, then He desires that you grow enough in your faith to trust and believe His Word. Perhaps He is planning to, as Deuteronomy 8:2 suggests, "test you, to know what was in your heart, whether you would keep His commandments or not." The will of the Lord for your life is contained in the words of the Bible. You don't need a direct revelation from Him to know His plan for you—it's all right there. When you actually sit down, communicate with Him in prayer and read His Word, you'll begin to see and understand Him. And the more you know about Him, the more you'll come to realize how well your relationship with Him prepares you to relate to others.

You've got to be completely clear on the fact that absolutely nothing can proceed in the area of your Christian marriage until you take the time to know Him who is creating it. Right now, let's take the time to look at some more Scriptures:

- Exodus 15:2. "The LORD is my strength and song, and He has become my salvation."
- Psalm 37:4. "Delight yourself also in the LORD, and He shall give you the desires of your heart."
- Psalm 37:23. "The steps of a good man are ordered by the LORD, and He delights in his way."
- Psalm 127:1. "Unless the LORD builds the house, they labor in vain who build it."
- Psalm 138:8. "The LORD will perfect that which concerns me."
- Proverbs 3:5. "Trust in the LORD with all your heart, and lean not on your own understanding."
- Proverbs 3:6. "In all your ways acknowledge Him, and He shall direct your paths."
- Proverbs 8:14. "Counsel is mine, and sound wisdom; I am understanding, I have strength."
- Psalm 119:151. "You are near, O LORD, and all Your commandments are truth."
- Proverbs 9:10. "The fear of the LORD is the beginning of wisdom, and the knowledge of the Holy One is understanding."
- Psalm 46:10. "Be still, and know that I am God."

The verses I've quoted are just a sample of the multitude of reassurances that God gives us in His Word, which clearly teaches that He is directing and guiding our lives. He is in control, and He knows what He is doing. If we fully understand who it is that holds our reins, we can confidently relax and follow. He won't lead us astray.

THE ENEMY'S DYNAMIC DUO

Depression and a sense of futility are the biggest obstacles you will face as you come to grips with the reality of God's timetable. We all believe, for some unknown reason, that we can hurry up or urge God along, or that we can beg and cajole Him into acting on something we desire. After we've done all that we can and have failed, we come to the realization that we are helpless. No matter how hard we try, we still can't accomplish our goals without God. This is often a hard lesson to learn. It is very easy to sink into a state of depression when the realization hits us. We cry, "What's the use?" We pout and accuse God of lying. We grumble, "You're never going to do it."

These are negative, destructive, self-fulfilling statements, and a marriage-minded woman has much better things to do than to waste her time trying to get back on track after the setbacks that these accusations will bring. Satan, however, would like nothing better than to see you wallow in them. Depression and the feeling of helplessness are two of the most effective weapons he has against the Christian woman, because too often we don't realize their source. We think it's "just me," and that feelings of depression, futility, and anger toward God for "withholding" from us our heart's desire are natural. These thoughts, however, are planted by Satan. They are among the most potent weapons in his arsenal, ones that he does not hesitate to use against us in an attempt to destroy our relationship with God. We must learn to see depression and futility for what they really are . . . Satan's arrows, specifically designed to kill, to steal, and to destroy.

Believe it or not, God is completely aware of how impatient you feel. However, your human scale perspective is so different from His that you cannot even begin to understand how

He views your life unless you see what He Himself has to say about it. If you will once again turn to His Word, you'll find insights there for dealing with the negative seeds that Satan is trying to harvest in you.

What Does God Say About . . .

Futility/Depression:

- Psalm 77:7. "Will the Lord cast off forever? And will He be favorable no more?"
- Job 6:8. "Oh, that I might have my request, that God would grant me the thing that I long for!"
- Psalm 69:3. "I am weary with my crying; my throat is dry; my eyes fail while I wait for my God."
- Psalm 6:3. "My soul also is greatly troubled; but You, O LORD—how long?"
- Psalm 38:17. "For I am ready to fall, and my sorrow is continually before me."
- Psalm 6:6. "I am weary with my groaning; all night I make my bed swim; I drench my couch with my tears."

Faith—The Antidote:

- Psalm 145:14. "The LORD upholds all who fall, and raises up all who are bowed down."
- Psalm 138:3. "In the day when I cried out, You answered me, and made me bold with strength in my soul."
- Psalm 62:8. "Trust in Him at all times, you people; pour out your heart before Him; God is a refuge for us."
- Psalm 57:2. "I will cry out to God Most High, to God who performs all things for me."
- Psalm 55:22. "Cast your burden on the LORD, and He shall sustain you."
- Psalm 34:17. "The righteous cry out, and the LORD hears, and delivers them out of all their troubles."
- Psalm 30:5. "Weeping may endure for a night, but joy comes in the morning."

Patience—The Fruit:

- Psalm 40:1. "I waited patiently for the LORD; and He inclined to me, and heard my cry."
- Lamentations 3:25. "The LORD is good to those who wait for Him, to the soul who seeks Him."
- Psalm 33:20. "Our soul waits for the LORD; He is our help and our shield."
- Isaiah 30:18. "Therefore the LORD will wait, that He may be gracious to you; . . . Blessed are all those who wait for Him."
- Isaiah 40:31. "But those who wait on the LORD shall renew their strength; they shall mount up with wings like eagles, they shall run and not be weary, they shall walk and not faint."
- Psalm 27:14. "Wait on the LORD; be of good courage, and He shall strengthen your heart; wait, I say, on the LORD!"

Be sure to read through the above passages from the Bible several times, or as many times as it takes to clearly understand that:

1. Although depression and futility will strike you, God says that your faith, demonstrated by your patient waiting, will overcome them.

2. The Lord will strengthen and sustain you while you wait.

3. God will move and bring your hopes and desires to pass in His appointed time.

It is all too easy to become weary with praying and waiting for a specific event to occur, in this case, for your promised husband to arrive. But, if God has said it will come to pass, it is already done. We are greatly limited by our inability to see more than one day at a time. Although we can anticipate what will happen in the next minute, hour, day, or week, we cannot see ahead and know for sure. God, on the other hand, is omniscient. He knows all and sees all. He does not view time and events in a straight line, as we do, because He sees everything from an eternal perspective. Let's take a visual look at this attribute of God:

YOUR VISION: GOD'S VISION:

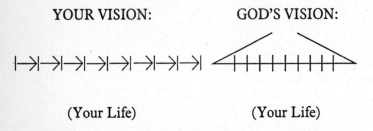

(Your Life)   (Your Life)

As this illustration shows, as far as God is concerned, with His view of the overall picture, the events in your life that you are so fervently praying for are already answered. He knows who your husband is, on what day you will marry, the dates when any future children will arrive, and so on with all the experiences that lie ahead of you. People say, "I don't see it," but God says, "It is already done." Your faith is what lets you believe that.

Second Peter 3:8 tells us, "With the Lord one day is as a thousand years, and a thousand years as one day." Fortunately, because your life span will be nowhere near that long, the events you anticipate in your life will not take nearly so long to occur. In order to see them arrive, however, you must stay steadfast on the pathway the Lord has set for you, from now on. The past has already gone. As for the future, no matter how much you may have veered from God's will earlier in your life, you must commit yourself to stay the course now. You are a Christian, and letting God lead you should become first-nature to you.

Galatians 6:9 states, "Let us not grow weary while doing good, for in due season we shall reap if we do not lose heart." An essential component of "doing good" is praying, seeking, and following the Word of God. First Corinthians 15:58 instructs us to be "steadfast, immovable, always abounding in the work of the Lord." Hebrews 3:14 states, "For we have become partakers of Christ if we hold the beginning of our confidence steadfast to the end." In case you're not sure, steadfast means to be "faithful, steady, firm, and established." In other words, don't give up and don't quit. No matter how long it takes or how slowly things seem to be going, the Lord's will is being worked out in your life, as long as you maintain your submission to Him. Be confident that you are moving forward, one day at a time, to the day when you will arrive at your goal.

GOALS, GOALS, GOALS

Believe it or not, marriage is not the only, or even the ultimate goal that the Lord has for your life. While you concentrate on this one thing, it is very easy to forget about all the other wonderful plans that God has in store for you; but, by doing so, you will only hold yourself back. You will find it highly beneficial, while you idle on hold, to seek His will about these other goals also.

Take time to communicate with God and to concentrate on seeing that His plans bear fruit in every area of your life. You'll gain some much needed perspective by simply stepping back and ceasing to single-mindedly focus on marriage. You were not created solely to be an appendage to a husband. You are not a half person waiting to become whole. You are complete in Jesus. He has made you whole, even if you never marry in the physical realm. You, as well as every other Christian, male or female, are the Bride of Christ. You are joined to the Lord, and are, therefore, spiritually and physically complete.

Often, single women idealize the state of marriage as being blissful and perfect. They fantasize that when they marry all their problems will be solved, and all questions answered; that their lives will then go forward, focused and centered around another human being. By painting such a lovely, though false, picture of marriage, they set themselves up for great disappointment when a man, a markedly human man, with all his frailties intact, enters their lives. No one can ever live up to the glorious images we women can frame in our minds.

The point is that you are a unique and beautiful person in your own right. You are the pearl we talked about earlier, and God has put you into the world, and saved and delivered you for a reason. Believe it or not, marriage is *not* the reason you are here. No matter where you are on the timetable of your life, whether you are in a relationship or not, you must set aside space and time in your life to find out God's purpose and plan for you, and do whatever you must to help Him bring it to fruition. I know it sounds strange, in a book for marriage-minded single Christian women, to state that marriage is not what you should be seeking, but that is exactly the truth. You must seek God and His will for every area of your life, for your life does not begin or end with marriage. Hopefully, you have many, many days ahead of you; use each of them to bring honor and glory to the Lord and to bless others.

As Habakkuk 2:3 states, "For the vision is yet for an appointed time; but at the end it will speak, and it will not lie. Though it tarries, wait for it; because it will surely come, it will not tarry." Stay the course and be assured; everything is right on schedule in God's timetable.

Part 2

YOU AND GOD'S PLAN OF ACTION

"Ask, and it will be given to you; seek, and you will find; knock, and it will be opened to you."

Matthew 7:7

Introduction

How to Do It

A few chapters back, I mentioned that there are actions you can take that will greatly enhance your chances of being found by the Christian man of your dreams. These options are worth exploring at this point, because they are the kind of concrete actions that provide you with creative ways to expend energy in the matrimonial arena, while you still let God control the outcome. They don't involve taking the matter away from God's hands, but they do involve keeping your own hands busy; for if you're like me, waiting idly is nearly impossible. The key is to make moves or take steps that involve changing, improving, and developing yourself, because you are all you really have to work with. You will also be pleasantly surprised to find that getting off your "seat of do-nothing" will greatly help to free you from depression and futility, as long as it is God-ordained action. God is not opposed to your taking action if it is not destructive or contrary to His Word. According to Proverbs 16:9, "A man's heart plans his way, but the LORD directs his steps." Just remember to remain prayerful and actively committed to practicing the basics that we have already covered in Part 1.

Chapter 6

Get a Life

Are you bored? Do you consider yourself boring? Unexciting? Uninteresting? Do you wish to attract a boring, dull, unstimulating man? If you were a man, would you find yourself to be bland or colorless? Do you think that being drab is a Christian virtue? It is sad but true in many instances that Christian women feel that being a good Christian means subduing their personalities, their interests, and their abilities. Not so. God came into your life to enhance it, to stimulate and build your uniqueness, to bring out your hidden talents, and to make your life blossom and flourish.

Take time to investigate your creativity, to ponder and identify the potential God has put in you. What are your dreams, outside of those that pertain to marriage? Think about the activities you enjoy, and the inclinations and desires that lie quietly in the back of your mind. What are the activities that you really enjoy or think you could learn to enjoy? What talents has God given you? Do you sing, write, or draw? Do you love animals or babies? What about money? Unless you are independently wealthy, you probably need to work. What would you really like to do as a career? Do you harbor a secret wish to be a lawyer, interior designer, or talk show host? Do you want to preach or become a missionary?

These are all possible God-given seeds, dormant within you until you take steps to develop them.

Take out a sheet of paper and get your pen. (Don't do this in pencil—it's too easy to erase.) You are going to write a "bent" list. Your bent toward something is a God-given inclination to grow in a certain direction. It represents your most natural direction, because you are already leaning toward it.

Take the time right now to list everything that comes to your mind that you feel an inclination toward, no matter how far-fetched it may seem. Your list does not have to include Christian goals. God did not call everyone to be a foreign missionary, preacher, or Bible scholar. There's room in His kingdom, and a need in the world, for God's people to bring His perspective into all areas of the workplace. His perspective is particularly important in your life if He has given you abilities to positively influence or change people's lives. God needs Christian doctors, lawyers, police officers, counselors, politicians, and schoolteachers. There is plenty of His work to be done in those vocations, as well as any other you might want to pursue. Maybe you really would prefer to open your own business, perhaps a specialty store, a day care center, or a travel agency. Do you want to become proficient on the computer or learn accounting?

Be sure to include on your bent list any hobbies or activities that you enjoy, other than vegging out in front of the television. What? You say you haven't got any? Well, why not? If you haven't discovered anything to attract your interest, it may be because you have limited yourself so much that you haven't even gotten around to investigating activities to see if they might be fun for you. Have you tried your hand at tennis or bicycling? Do you like to play cards, or bowl, or sing in the choir? Have you ever thought about learning gourmet cooking, or painting, or photography? Write them all down. Don't worry about whether other Christians will understand or approve of the things on your list; this is your own personal catalog of interests. Don't preedit it to fit anyone else's standards. There are no judgments to be made on the rightness or wrongness of your interests by anyone but you and God. Never fear. If God is opposed to something you may want to do, you won't do it, because it will make you feel uncomfortable and ill at ease. But, let Him be the one to judge; don't limit yourself and your interests at this point. Let's list and evaluate them instead.

Now, on another sheet of paper, separate and organize the list. Make three columns, titled: (1) "Things I Already Do"; (2) "Things I Could Easily Do"; and (3) "Things About Which I Haven't a Clue." Break out your list accordingly. For most people, the "Things I Already Do" list is probably the shortest. It usually contains a small list of hobbies, pastimes, or interests; but, just look at the other two lists, and all the things you could be doing. They should be pretty impressive to you. Look at all that potential you've got lying dormant. Now, let's further refine the lists. Get out three more sheets, and write the title of a column as the heading on each one. It's time to consider how to move the lists into action.

LIST 1

On the "Things I Already Do" sheet, list your activities down the left side, with three or four lines between them. Adjacent to each activity, write out at least two things you might do to enhance and develop it. Let's say you bowl. Next to "bowling," you could write "join a bowling league" or "organize a bowling club at church." Don't limit your development listing only to what you will actually pursue. Write down whatever comes to mind that you could do. Suppose, on your list, you have "love animals." Have you considered volunteering to work with the animal shelter; getting a degree in veterinary medicine; opening a pet hotel; or joining or forming a cat or dog or fish lovers club?

How about "sing in the choir"? You could write "take voice lessons"; "perfect two or three songs in which I could

sing lead"; "form a duet or trio with other choir members."
This can be done for every interest and activity you are
currently involved in. No matter how insignificant it may
seem to be, if you enjoy doing it, put it on your list. There is
great creative potential in your interests. They are like tender
young buds that can blossom into hardy plants with nurtur-
ing. If left untended, they will not grow.

LIST 2

Now, let's consider your second list—"Things I Could
Easily Do." These are the activities you are not actively
pursuing, but which, by expending some effort, you could
start participating in almost immediately. They are easily
within the realm of possibility. This list probably contains a
host of things you have idly thought about doing, but have
been too busy (or too lazy) to pursue. For instance, maybe
you've always thought it might be fun to go horseback riding.
Well, how would you get started? You could check the phone
book for stables that give riding lessons; find out how much
it costs and set aside the money; take the lesson; or, you might
simply find a place that offers horseback riding and go for a
ride. Write down the steps, as suggested above, that you need
to take to pursue the things that you could easily do.

The point of this list is not to make a big project of the
activity, but to show you how simple it would be to get busy and
do it. Perhaps you're curious about the opera or ballet. What
must you do to feed your curiosity? Buy a ticket and go to a
ballet or opera. It's something you can easily do. Maybe you're
interested in writing. Pick up a piece of paper and pencil.
Chinese cooking—call a cooking school or buy a good recipe
book; painting—go to an art supply store and browse around.
There you can find books on various painting techniques, pick
up and examine painting materials, then study the bulletin
board that shows where art lessons are being offered.

Do this brainstorming for everything you currently have
on the list, and be sure to add whatever comes to mind later.

This is not a static or dead list—it is as vital and alive with possibilities as your relationship with God is. He has given it to you.

LIST 3

Now, it's time to take up list number three—the biggie. These are the things you have an interest in, but have considered to be either beyond your reach or too difficult or complicated to bring forth in your life. They are probably more career- or lifestyle-oriented than the other two lists, and will include goals that other people might consider far-fetched or impossible. Don't fall victim to negative thinking and decide to share their opinion. Remember, if God gave you the sincere desire, He gave you the potential and the ability to reach these goals. This ability may be long dormant or completely undeveloped, but it's still there. If you have the will to work, His will is to bring it to pass.

Don't handicap Him by your unbelief. Keep in mind the verse in Luke 17:6 about having faith as small as a mustard seed. God says that's all it takes. There are going to be a number of preliminary steps, and much preparation and work involved, because these are long-term objectives; but, if you will stay on the course, you can reach the goal. Nothing is impossible with God. At this point, we will list the objectives and evaluate how they might be brought to pass. Prayer and dedication will be necessary as you begin to move forward with your goals.

Just as you have done with the previous lists, it is necessary to list your interests down the left margin of a sheet of paper. Then take as much time and as much paper as you need to think through how you can begin to activate them. One very good way to begin is to break the end result down to the very first step that comes to mind. When this step is taken, other steps will reveal themselves as they become necessary. You don't have to have an entire outline ready before you can get from Point A to Point Z, but you must be able to evaluate what options exist at Point A. As you progress from there, you will begin to see and understand what constitutes Point B, and the steps you need to take to get there. As you move toward your ultimate goal, each step will present itself more clearly, and you will begin to pick up speed. You'll be just like a snowball heading down a hill, gathering size and velocity, and becoming more proficient as you go.

Don't be afraid to list even the simplest steps you can take to reach your goals. Remember that if you don't have a beginning, it is impossible to reach a destination. Think of yourself as sitting in St. Louis, your Point A. In one direction, there's San Francisco; another direction leads to Los Angeles, another to New York, or Miami, or Houston, or Chicago. How do you get there? Well, the first step, of course, is to decide where you want to go, and in the case of the goals on your third list, your life will be much simpler if you pick one destination at a time. You must then point yourself in the right direction and head toward the nearest town. If you follow a road from one town to the next, always heading in the proper direction, you will eventually reach your city, your Point Z.

Of course, it would help immeasurably to have a road map of some sort. Then your entire route could be laid out, clearly and simply, ready for you to just forge ahead. However, on the road of our lives, God seldom gives us a map. He desires, instead, that we trust in Him and pray. Keep the goal in sight and take one step at a time. He knows the route. But, we do have to start the car and drive. It would be quite interesting to see how you would get to a destination if you never left your house.

It's time to consider some "for instances." At this point, during the list formation stage, we are primarily concerned with Step 1—getting the car started and out of the driveway. Let's take a fairly easy example to follow: You'd really like to become a doctor. Never mind that you're forty years old and have never been in a hospital except during an appendicitis attack. Keep in mind that if you feel a real desire, and not just a passing fancy, the ability to accomplish your goal already resides inside you. Your first step at Point A would be to call around and investigate the requirements for getting into medical school. Point B would involve considering financial options.

In fact, with most career-oriented goals, some type of specialized training is probably involved, even if you are just brimming over with innate ability. That ability must be channeled and focused. Your first step will almost always require that you identify the necessary training or experience needed, and acquire it. If you want to open your own restaurant, you would be wise to work in one for a while in order to gain firsthand knowledge. If the glamour and glitter of being a television announcer beckons you, there are a number of entry-level positions you will probably have to hold first. They will pay much less and not provide the level of exposure that the glamour position to which you aspire does. Any sort of job at your local television or radio station, even if it's a receptionist position, will open the door, and give you a start on the road to your goal. The first step following Point A always takes us out of the fantasy realm and into reality. That's when you decide whether or not this is really the direction you want to take; if you want to stick with it and run the course, or if you'd really rather head for Chicago instead.

TALENTS

I hope that by now you have at least jotted down your preliminary bent list. If not, stop right now and do it. Perhaps you're stalled, wondering "How will this help me get a husband?" NO, NO, NO. What we are trying to do is help you establish a life for yourself. The focus is not on a man, but on you, your talents, and your God-given gifts. Reevaluate the parable Jesus told about the talents in Matthew 25:14–30. On a very literal level, God requires that you use and develop the talents He has given you. He is extremely displeased if you bury them—they provide the key to increased riches and treasure, materially, spiritually, and emotionally. He has given these abilities to you. He truly does expect that you will nurture and develop them. There is a very apt summation of the situation in the phrase, "use it or lose it." You will also note in the parable that the servants of God who used their talents gained even more from God than they had developed on their own. When we expand and develop one talent, we uncover still others that we barely knew we had. There are all kinds of dividends waiting to be reaped by those of us willing to do our very best with the gifts God has given us.

Don't worry about the kind of talents God has given you. Nor should you compare yourself with others, and like the unfaithful servant in the parable, become concerned that you were given only one talent. He developed a resentful attitude, and spitefully decided that his one talent was not worth using at all, so he buried it and then gave it back to his master untouched. What a negative attitude. It is unworthy of a Christian. Whatever talents or gifts God has given you have been given for you to use to develop and prosper. Don't worry that you can't see the final outcome that awaits the use of your talent. Your task is to get out there and make the effort. The outcome is in God's hands. Proverbs 18:16 states that "A man's gift makes room for him, and brings him before great men." In other words, your abilities *will* be recognized by other people but only when you use them.

In addition to your natural talents, God has also given you spiritual gifts. Take time to investigate all of the specific gifts that He has implanted within the church. Each Christian has one or more of them, each of which is designed to bless and strengthen the body of Christ. First Corinthians 12 provides an extensive outline of these gifts, and you'll find a number of excellent books in your Christian bookstore that explore God's spiritual gifts in detail. You'll find that identifying and developing your spiritual gifts will greatly aid your growth and fulfillment as a fully functioning member of both the local and universal church body.

As for the husband, think about it for a moment. Surely, you realize that a happy, productive, active person is far more attractive to a potential mate than is a sad, bored one, afflicted with a terminal case of the mopes. Developing and pursuing goals that are important to you will not only energize you and work wonders for your disposition; you will be amazed at the number of new people who will be drawn into your life. Although few of them will be marital candidates, they are still there for a reason. God wants you to pray for their salvation, and to be a witness to them, a living testimony of His saving grace. The more people you come into contact with, the greater the fruits of His harvest. If you look at it from God's perspective, it becomes even more imperative that you expend the time and effort necessary to fully use what He has given you. There are lives at stake.

Now, review your lists. There should be several activities that interest you enough to start on immediately. Don't forget to pray for God's direction and blessings first, then go for it.

Chapter 7

The Friendliness Factor

Another area of your life that you can set your hand to, with God's complete approval, is developing friendships. As we discussed in the last chapter, you will find that as you begin to pursue the interests and abilities that God has given you, lots of other people will be drawn into your pathway. Contrary to your possibly cynical beliefs, you were not put here to stroll solemnly down a straight and narrow path, alone with God, marching into the sunset. That's not at all what He planned for your life. The very fact that you desire marriage indicates a God-given urge to share your life with others. As you proceed down the road God has set you on, you'll find other people entering, exiting, and crossing your path in all kinds of ways. If you take the time to talk to and get to know them, these people can enrich your life with countless blessings, just as you can positively impact theirs. We're going to take time here to consider some frequently asked questions on friendship.

WHAT CAN FRIENDSHIPS DO FOR ME?

Intimacy

God blesses us with friendships, not simply for our own personal edification, but also to develop and build into us the capacity for intimacy. On a personal level, having friends to share with will prove to be a source of comfort to you during the mate wait. Friends can lend support, help rally sagging spirits, or provide much needed listening posts. Unlike some of our relatives, most friends will make an effort not to be judgmental or negative, and can help clarify our direction. Proverbs 18:24 calls a good friend one "who sticks closer than a brother."

On a deeper level, interaction with friends can serve to mirror and enhance your relationship with God. The capacity for intimacy between two people; the empathy and sharing that takes place; the exposure of our true selves, our emotions and desires, successes and disappointments, and even our secrets, all serve to build connections between us and others. What we learn to share with friends is also what we need to share with God in our intimate relationship with Him. Sometimes, this works in the opposite direction. Often people are quite comfortable pouring out their hearts to God, but have not learned the comforts of doing the same thing with a good friend. It is very easy for a single woman to become emotionally bottled up if she has no intimate conversational outlet. God wants us to maintain a healthy balance. We need to have both personal interaction and spiritual interaction in our lives.

God has given us numerous examples of close friendships in the Bible; for example, the bond between Ruth and Naomi in the book of Ruth, or David and Jonathan in 1 Samuel. In the New Testament, we read about Jesus and His friends, Mary, Martha, and Lazarus; and the relationship between Paul and Silas and other members of the Corinthian church. These are important illustrations of how vital to our lives the bonds of filial love really are. The other two kinds of love, *eros* (physical), and *agape* (spiritual), are very special, but *philia* (brotherly) love is essential in facilitating the development of intimacy in our daily living.

Practice Makes Perfect

Taking the initiative to build up the friendships in your life is also an extremely constructive way to take action in the marriage arena. Your willingness to reveal yourself and to share with others, to be open and receptive enough to allow others into your life, is great training for allowing a real friendship to form with the man God will bring into your life. You will need to build true emotional intimacy with him prior to marriage. Learning to share your inner self with him is one of the best of all assurances that you will avoid the superficial, "surface only" nature of so many marriages in the world that end up in divorce court.

The give and take that we learn in any close friendship prepares us to listen and compromise with, support, and enjoy the companionship of our mate. Also, keep in mind that when you marry, you'll not only be bringing into your life a husband, but in-laws, distant relatives, current and future children, and a host of assorted friends and coworkers. You'll be well-advised to develop your interpersonal skills, because maintaining friendly relationships with this multitude will be essential to maintaining peace and harmony in your married life.

Variety

God has created several billion people to populate this earth. And, each one is different. As a Christian, you should already have discovered that just as you contain a wealth of possibilities, so does everyone else. Many of the people you will meet, while pursuing your new goals and activities, are potential Christians. Since it is only God who knows for sure who will or will not be added to His flock, you must never arbitrarily discount the value of a person, just because he or she is not a practicing Christian. Each and every person who enters your life has the potential to enhance it. Leave yourself open to the discovery of the uniqueness in others. Even if you and another person will never be close friends, there should be room in your life for casual friendships and acquaintances.

Help—I'm Shy

For most people, making friends is not a major problem. However, if you are shy or bashful, you may have to put forth extra effort. Don't just sit back and expect people to come running over, fascinated by your mere presence, and anxious to be your friend. People who sow the seeds of friendship are the ones who reap it. Proverbs 18:24 states, "A man who has friends must himself be friendly." It's not hard to do, no matter how shy or introverted you may be. You'll be surprised what a pleasant smile or a friendly greeting can accomplish.

It's an easy enough thing to get used to doing. The next time you meet a stranger, put a smile on your face, make eye contact, and say hello. Try to do it every time you meet someone. Most likely a conversation will ensue, and you will have just taken a significant step toward developing a new friendship. If you keep working at meeting others, you may even find yourself developing a taste for it. To a large degree, friendliness reproduces itself. A smile begets a smile, a pleasant hello generates an amiable response. It may be tempting to sit quietly in the corner among the houseplants, while everyone else seems to be enjoying themselves, but you will be depriving yourself of the very interactions that can build your confidence. Get out there and smile. No one is going to bite!

Well, I'm Not

Whether shyness is a special problem for you or not, you should be concerned about the quality of your friendships. Quantity is an irrelevant factor. It is more important that no matter how many or how few people you know, you have at least one intimate friend. One or two friends is optimal, since the type of sharing common in a very close relationship should be limited to those special people whom you wholeheartedly trust.

As friends, both you and those you are close to must be extremely careful never to divulge confidences to others. Proverbs 17:9 warns that "he who repeats a matter separates friends." Proverbs 11:13 states, "A talebearer reveals secrets, but he who is of a faithful spirit conceals a matter." The intimate relationship you develop with a close friend is so special that its confidences must never be broken.

A word here is appropriate on the subject of gossip. God never intended for what the dictionary defines as "idle discussion of rumors about others" to be a component of friendship. However, in many relationships, idle or even malicious gossip is an essential component. You must be extremely careful to never let your friendships degenerate to that level— God hates gossip. Proverbs 10:31 tells us that "The mouth of the righteous brings forth wisdom, but the perverse [uncontrolled, stubbornly willful] tongue will be cut out." Proverbs 13:3 offers God's ultimate decree for gossip: "He who guards his mouth preserves his life, but he who opens wide his lips shall have destruction." Truly, that's something worth considering.

All of these attributes of friendship reflect the quality of your friendships. A truly close friend should share your values and understand what makes you tick. The Bible directs us, as Christians, to put away the things of the world, and that includes close friendships with people who are not Christians. This doesn't mean that you suddenly stop speaking to the woman who's been your best friend since you were both in grade school. You are perfectly free to continue to associate with her, but you will find that the more your faith develops, the less you'll have in common with her on a deeper level.

As for acquaintances and casual friends, there are few restrictions other than the ones that your own comfort level permits. Enjoy these people for who they are and keep them lifted up in prayer. Just be careful never to let them sway you from God's purpose and plan for your life. In Proverbs 14:7 you are instructed to "Go from the presence of a foolish man, when you do not perceive in him the lips of knowledge." Your prayers will reap dividends for both you and your non-Christian friend. Job 42:10 states that "The LORD restored Job's losses when he prayed for his friends. Indeed the LORD gave

Job twice as much as he had before." These blessings came to Job when he began to intercede to God for his friends. Remember, that is probably why God brought your friends to you in the first place. Lift them up daily in intercessory prayer.

HOSPITALITY—THE BRIDGE BUILDER

As a single Christian woman, you will primarily meet people either in church, at church-related activities, or at work. Now that you've added an abundant supply of extra-curricular activities to your schedule, you'll also come into contact with a flow of newcomers from those sources. You may be starting to wonder what you're supposed to do with them all.

This may or may not come as a surprise, but God directs that we be "given to hospitality." According to the diction-ary, hospitality means "generosity and friendliness in the entertainment of guests." However, the Bible's original definition extends this definition to include strangers. In 1 Timothy 3:2 and Titus 1:8, it is stated that a bishop or deacon of the church is required to be "hospitable." In 1 Peter 4:9 we read that we should be "hospitable to one another without grumbling." Romans 12:13 also directs us to be "given to hospitality." The definition of hospitality can be expanded to include the sharing of our time and energy on behalf of another. Being pleasant, kind, considerate, and hospitable are Christian virtues.

How can you do it? Try spending time with people. Make the effort to invite them to your home; keep abreast of birthdays, or the need for a wedding shower or a baby shower. Bring a platter of your special desserts or a loaf of freshly baked bread to the people in your department. Take time to find the right greeting card or small, special gift for a person who is going through a painful time.

The best way to perfect your entertaining skills is by doing; investigate the techniques for giving a simple party or a get-together, and give one. You'll be surprised to know how many people are seeking a place to go on holidays or weekends. Don't set yourself up to always be a guest or to put your role as hostess on hold until you become someone's wife. Instead, get with a friend to share resources and information, and cohost a gathering for any reason you choose. How about a regular home Bible study, a Sunday brunch after church, or a patio barbecue? You'll find plenty of ideas if you look for them.

If you don't feel motivated to entertain extensively in your home, your very own church can supply a highly appreciative application of your hospitality skills. Almost all churches need ushers and hostesses, welcoming committees, and volunteers to visit sick people and shut-ins. Many offer bereavement committees to cook and care for families and friends at funerals, or wedding coordinators to oversee arrangements for weddings held at the church. There are any number of opportunities available for you to put your hospitable inclinations to good use.

Why should you bother? Because the practice of hospitality is simply a natural extension of friendliness. You'll find that "breaking bread" with people is one of the best ways to bond with them. The Bible endorses it. What do you think the Last Supper was? Among other things, it was a confirmation of the bond of friendship between Jesus and His disciples.

Take a look at the hospitality Jesus demonstrated when He changed the water into wine at the wedding in Canaan; or when He went to dinner at the house of Zacchaeus, or even to the homes of a variety of "publicans and sinners." The barriers of understanding between the God-man and the people He came to save were broken down as He supped with them and partook of their hospitality. You'll find that the barriers between you and others will start to crumble when you, in like manner, offer them the opportunity to partake of your God-given hospitality.

So, as we close out this chapter, have you begun to grasp the reasons that friendships are important in your life, not just old friends but new ones for whom God has an extra special purpose? Your newer friendships are likely to bring a big change from the old patterns in your life, because God has changed and renewed you. The new people He brings into your life will enhance and develop the Christian virtues of the new you.

Now, I must share one final word of caution that God gives straight from His Word. As you get out and socialize the Bible warns against overstaying your welcome. God, who is concerned with every aspect of our lives, cares enough even to be concerned about that. He wants us to be sensitive enough about what is going on with people around us to pick up the clues that can tell us when "enough is enough." Proverbs 25:17 phrases this in a most succinct manner by advising, "Seldom set foot in your neighbor's house, lest he become weary of you and hate you."

Now go and have fun. Consider your practice of Christian hospitality to be yet another activity that can enhance your rapidly filling life. Yes, God does give you permission to do it. Friendships are in His plan for the full Christian life.

And . . . In Summation

Just in case you've forgotten or chosen to ignore what we've discussed in this section, those very important practical actions that are designed to get you off your sofa and into an active mode, here's a brief summation of what we've covered so far. Now you truly cannot say you didn't know.

- Write down your bent list of talents, gifts, and inclinations, then categorize them into the areas you can begin to work on now, the ones you can follow up on, and the ones you need to research and develop.
- Place a value upon and learn to cultivate the friendships in your life. They will expand your perspective in all kinds of ways.

- God has called us to practice hospitality. The Word of God would never have given hospitality such attention had He not considered it a vital activity for us to pursue. Accept that the admonition to be hospitable is included in that Word, and proceed forward from there.

These are really very small actions for you to take, but since they are God-ordained ones, you'll be thrilled to discover the positive impact they will have upon your life. As with everything in the Word of God, you have only to try it in order to see the rewards in your very own life. Move forward . . . stop procrastinating. You have nothing to lose and a multitude of friendships await you.

Chapter 8

Blind Dates Are Great

Contrary to the opinion of many women, I feel it is worth your time and effort to make the very best of the occasional blind date that may come your way as a by-product of friendship. For a seriously marriage-minded woman the potential benefits of blind dating cannot be overlooked. You risk little and stand to gain a great deal.

Although most everybody has her share of horror stories to tell, there are just as many successes around. However, few people mention their really great blind dates. It is much more interesting to tell everyone about the incredibly bad ones. Don't let all the negative talk or perhaps even an occasional bad experience dissuade you. A thoughtfully arranged blind date has exceptional potential, since the arranger has the benefit of being already acquainted with both parties and presumably an inside track to their likes and dislikes. Hopefully, her judgment is as good as her intentions.

There is little else to be discussed on this subject. It is included here simply to remind you and to reassure you that arranged dating is permissible for you as a Christian, and is even preferable to some of the other date-gathering options that exist.

Approach blind dates with a positive attitude and you'll usually have a pleasant time, even if the man turns out to be somewhat less than you expected. One option to consider if you are hesitant to go out on a date with a man you don't know is to suggest that you and he be introduced in the home of your mutual friend. If that is a bit too formal for your taste, you and your friend can always plan some sort of small gathering that will create the opportunity for the two of you to meet. In fact, "at a friend's house" ranks among singles as one of the top places to meet romantic possibilities.

So, if the opportunity arises go ahead and give it a try. Consider blind dates as yet another mating option that the Lord has made available to you. Thank Him that another person is looking out for your interests, and try not to discourage your friends in their efforts, no matter how negative you might feel. Go ahead and make the most of the possibilities of meeting a new person. With God in the picture, you have nothing to lose.

Chapter 9

Stay Rooted Where You Are Planted

In the midst of pursuing a wonderful, new, more fulfilling life, you may have occasion to wonder if maybe you ought to change churches also. After all, in your newly expanded travels, you have possibly been exposed to an interesting new church, an exciting singles ministry, or a dynamic pastor who has peaked your interest. All of a sudden, the grass begins to look greener in another pasture.

As the title of this chapter implies, in my opinion, you would probably be better served by staying put at least for the time being. Let's take a closer look at some of the reasons why.

During a time in your life when many things may be changing and boundaries shifting, particularly if you have activated your bent list, the upheaval of leaving one church and settling into a new one can merely add to the confusion. We need reliable constants in our lives during periods of stress or change. The familiarity of your church which has hopefully served you well at least to this point, can be even more comforting as your life becomes uprooted and less stable in other areas.

You may be harboring unrealistic expectations for a new church, particularly if you are planning the move for a superficial reason; for example, because you spotted an especially attractive man there. Even if the move is being prompted by friendship, a change in churches should be carefully considered. We are often under the illusion that the people in a new church are more interesting or exciting, or that our mate is waiting to be uncovered there. They seldom are, and he rarely is.

Study the soil in the parable of the sower that Jesus told in Matthew 13:3–8. In one sense, the "good soil" is the heart and soul of the individual herself. In another equally applicable interpretation, the soil is the quality of the church in which the Christian is planted. Good soil will permit her to grow deep roots and bring forth good fruit, while shallow soil will prevent her from attaining her full God-ordained potential. If your current church can't supply the proper God-centered environment that will let you develop your relationship with Jesus Christ to its fullest extent, then, and only then, should you consider a move. Your only criterion for moving to a new church should be the presence of God in the place.

Your commitment to God includes setting your hand to the tasks He has laid out before you. Ninety-nine percent of the time, your Christian service will be connected to the needs that God has brought to your attention at your own church. He has placed you there because He has work for you to do there. Instead of trying to jump ship and climb aboard another vessel, you should be looking around for the tasks that need to be done right where you are. If the ship you're on isn't quite shipshape, what can *you* do to help fix it?

God frequently compares the church body and its pastor to a flock and its shepherd; and He holds the leader accountable for the souls He has given him. Let's look into the Word:

To Pastors

- 1 Peter 5:2–4. "Shepherd the flock of God which is among you, serving as overseers, not by compulsion but willingly, not for dishonest gain but eagerly; nor as being lords over those entrusted to you, but being examples to the flock; and when the Chief Shepherd appears, you will receive the crown of glory that does not fade away."

- Acts 20:28. "Therefore take heed to yourselves and to all the flock, among which the Holy Spirit has made you overseers, to shepherd the church of God which He purchased with His own blood."

To the Flock

- Hebrews 13:17. "Obey those who rule over you, and be submissive, for they watch out for your souls, as those who must give account. Let them do so with joy and not with grief, for that would be unprofitable for you."
- Ezekiel 34:11–12. "For thus says the Lord GOD: 'Indeed I Myself will search for My sheep and seek them out. As a shepherd seeks out his flock on the day he is among his scattered sheep, so will I seek out My sheep and deliver them from all the places where they were scattered on a cloudy and dark day.' "

Other sheep/shepherd analogies can be found in Psalm 23; Ezekiel 34; Zechariah 11; John 10; and in many other chapters of both the Old and New Testaments. There are so many verses available for study because God wants us to clearly understand that He is the one who places His sheep in flocks and holds His undershepherd, the pastor, responsible for them. Of course, you have your own free will, but leaving the care of your shepherd and wandering off in search of a new one must be done with the utmost caution. It may seem to be a light matter, but it is not. God must decide whether it is time for you to move. If so, you will have His blessing.

If it is not God's will for you to leave the church you attend, and you have been praying fervently for your special personal request, God may be getting ready to open up and pour out His blessing on you, but you could miss out if you have strayed away from your place. The shower descends onto an empty spot. Don't try to second-guess God; maybe you think you should move because your blessing might be awaiting you at the new church, but that's not God's way. He knows where He planted you, and He knows how to get His blessings to you, as long as you remain subject to His will. A hasty decision to switch churches could end up putting you outside His will, and thus jeopardize a swifter answer to your prayers. As my pastor once phrased it, "If you're not walking where God wants you to walk, don't expect Him to show up where you are."

Sometimes the inclination to make a change strikes because you become impatient. You begin to feel that God has buried you away in a church filled with married couples, families, and elderly people. It seems as if most every other church in town has more single members, and you're stalled on hold, in a place where you can't possibly meet a mate. You might then begin to consider trying a move to another church as a method of jump-starting God ... of maybe prodding Him into action. It won't work. God is smarter than you are and more aware than even your most devious subterfuge.

Be honest to yourself and to God about the process in operation here. He is running the entire show; settle down and wait. You'll not only receive the answer to your prayers more quickly that way, but you'll reap the rewards of learning patience as well. Stay where He has planted you; make a commitment to your flock and to your shepherd. And trust the Lord that He really does know what He is doing, even when you haven't a clue.

Chapter 10

What About the Personals?

Ⅰf you live in or near almost any large city, you've probably noticed what is becoming an increasingly prevalent phenomenon in the methodical nineties—the "personals" ad. All kinds of newspapers, specialty papers, and magazines carry columns of these personal solicitations for dates, mates, or sexual partners. And nestled among them are a rapidly growing number of ads placed by Christian men and women seeking Christian mates. Perhaps you have considered placing such an ad yourself, but you have questions about whether or not it is proper or permissible.

I have solicited the opinions of pastors and counselors as well as singles who have advertised, and I can only report mixed results. Uniformly, the Christian professionals regard personal ads with intense skepticism. They believe that advertising is yet another attempt to wrest control of the mating dilemma away from God and back into the hands of the individual. They hold that singles should wait on and trust in God for the arrival of their spouse-to-be. They also reject personal ads as being just another device to circumvent God, and they note that the Bible tells us to avoid worldly responses to our problems and situations.

Some Scriptures that appear to support their position include Romans 12:2; 2 Corinthians 6:17; Matthew 6:33; and Proverbs 4:14. However, it is important to note here that these same professionals, who are so opposed to ads, see nothing wrong with singles groups as long as they are sponsored by churches. The idea of getting single Christian men and women together is not objectionable as a concept. It becomes problematic when the singles involved step out on their own, outside the confines of the church, and attempt to locate each other one on one.

On the other hand, Christian singles who have ventured forth into the personals realm are generally optimistic, although few seem to have actually attracted the desired results. Most report that although they specifically sought Christian respondents, non-Christians were the predominant responders. Many of the people who answered their ads assumed a stance of Christianity by birth and did not feel at all excluded by the Christian requirement. Several of the advertising singles noted that "real" Christian singles seemed to not be reading personals ads or were hesitant about responding, if they read the ads at all.

Most had received no responses from true Christians. My inquiries were limited only to my local area, so the same may not be the case in your town. However, these singles found that the personals were much more productive as a potential mission field than they were at drawing out a mate. Still, none of the singles I spoke with has given up hope. As a group, they all seem to be outgoing, adventurous, friendly, and open to meeting new people. They viewed their personal ads as simply another permissible option for dating, which, with God's help and sufficient prayer, might actually bring forth that one special person. They voiced the attitude that they had "nothing to lose and everything to gain," particularly if their ad was carefully worded so as not to give a false picture of either themselves or their requirements.

The primary biblical justification in the minds of these singles who advertise for Christian mates seems to be that the Bible does not expressly forbid it. The ads fall into a gray category that reflects the specific era we inhabit. I can, however, insert at least one applicable Scripture here. If you truly believe that "The steps of a good man are ordered by the LORD" (Ps. 37:23), and if you have prayed and sought the Lord about the matter and received the go-ahead to answer a personal ad, neither I, nor anyone else, has the right to pronounce you wrong. As usual, the determining criteria is your prayer life and your relationship with God.

In most cases, the personals have proven to be primarily neutral—they have neither hurt nor particularly helped to advance the arrival of God's intended. They serve mainly as a means of increasing the number of people who populate your life, people to whom you can be a witness, or otherwise instrumental in increasing their awareness of God.

If you do choose to advertise, to respond to someone else's ad, or to use a dating service as a date enhancer, it must be done with the understanding that the people who enter your life via these avenues are not throwaways. You must devote the same amount of time and energy toward their salvation as you do for any other person who directly intersects your path. God brought them to you for a reason. Don't just say "No, you're not a Christian, and you aren't going to be my mate," and then walk away. Accept the responsibility for whoever enters your life. If you are bold and have enough faith in the Lord to advertise, then go ahead and accept the consequences. Few of your responses are going to be from actual marriage partners, but all will be from people you need to serve.

Chapter 11

The Importance of Staying Attractive

Take a closer look at this chapter title. It is another one I'm passing on to you just as the Lord gave it to me. The operative idea here is the word "staying." The Lord created you and He made you attractive. You may not be beautiful or pretty by the world's standards, but God made you an attractive person in your own right.

LET'S GET PHYSICAL

What I'm referring to in the chapter title is the fact that as the years pass, we seldom retain the degree of attractiveness God gave us. Much of that is inevitable. No one expects a thirty-five-year-old woman to look like an eighteen-year-old, just as few women would be interested in a fifty-two-year-old man trying to look or act like a twenty-five-year-old. We should not even want to remain unchanged by time. Aging is truly a process of getting better, of maturing, of developing depth of character, soul, and personality, as well as our own personal style.

The concept of staying attractive does not mean staying just as we have always been, of fossilizing ourselves in place, of never changing our "look" for fear that someone will realize that we have gotten older. Rather, staying attractive operates on the opposite assumption. We accept the fact that we are changing, but we also acknowledge that at each age and stage of our life, we have the potential to be an attractive person, albeit in a slightly revised manner. It means making the effort to look your very best no matter what your age. It is a reflection of your self-esteem and confidence rather than a subjective measure of physical beauty. Every woman can be attractive if she makes the effort. It's simply a matter of being the best you can be and doing the most with whatever God has given you.

Now, clear from your head the false notion that if a Christian woman takes care of her appearance she is vain, and vanity is a sin. By this line of thought, the uglier or less attractive a woman is, the better a Christian she is. God never said that. It is nowhere to be found in the Bible, and fortunately, because of its lack of biblical basis, few pastors hold to the concept today.

Our primary concern is usually with defining and becoming our very best self. Exactly what does that mean? It's easy to find out—your mirror will tell you. Which things about yourself have you begun to let slip? Maybe you've always watched your diet, but now, you've ballooned up with thirty pounds of extra fat. Were you always careful to keep your clothing well groomed, but now everything you put on is either too small or has a safety pin holding it together?

Here are some more things to consider. Do you keep your body clean? Your food healthy? Your makeup tasteful? Have you determined what clothing styles best flatter you, and tried to add them to your wardrobe as finances permit? How about that weight? If you can't be happy with yourself because of the poundage you are carrying around, do something about it. Procrastination is destructive to both your health and your self-esteem. What about that exercise program you've been intending to start? When do you plan to get moving?

If you realize something is not quite right with you and your appearance, you are the only one who can do something about it. God does not function as a fairy godmother—He will not come in, wave a wand and fix you up, transforming you into a beautiful princess. You must take the time to care for and to value yourself. You were created a woman, and you should rejoice in and make the most of that fact. Men do. Your femininity and personal attractiveness are potent draws for garnering attention from the opposite sex. And how you feel about yourself is clearly reflected in your outward appearance. You are not helpless or at the mercy of forces outside your control. Take control of yourself, your life, and your body. Try to make it a goal to never look less than your best. It is not a manifestation of vanity or pride, but rather, it is a form of honoring God by taking the best possible care of His temple—your own self. Some Scriptures that support the care of oneself include 1 Corinthians 6:15, 20 and chapters 5 and 6 of the Song of Solomon, with their praises to the "fairest" of women.

THE MAN FACTOR

Don't let yourself be fooled. A woman's physical appearance ranks very high on most men's true criteria for selecting their mates. Fortunately, few guys require that their woman be a stunning beauty. It is sufficient that he finds her physically appealing. Also fortunate is the fact that men have very different standards for attractiveness, just as women do when evaluating men.

Take an honest look at yourself, determine what it will take for you to look your very best, then proceed with it. If you need help, call in the specialists. It is particularly important to consult a doctor if you need guidance on diet or exercise, but there are also people out there who can get your hair in order, or show you how to use makeup knowledgeably, or how to coordinate your wardrobe. They are all readily available to you. Go ahead and get yourself taken care of—God has no objections.

. . . AS BEAUTY DOES

I'm sure you knew this was coming despite our initial focus on appearance. Inner beauty is just as vital as outward beauty. Let's investigate the validity of the phrase, "beauty is as beauty does." This is not a biblical quote, so let's see what the Bible has to say on the matter:

- Proverbs 11:16. "A gracious woman retains honor . . ."
- Proverbs 11:22. "As a ring of gold in a swine's snout, so is a lovely woman who lacks discretion."
- Proverbs 31:25–26. "Strength and honor are her clothing; . . . She opens her mouth with wisdom, and on her tongue is the law of kindness."
- Galatians 5:22–23. "The fruit of the Spirit is love, joy, peace, longsuffering, kindness, goodness, faithfulness, gentleness, self-control."

As an additional illustration, I also highly recommend that you read the book of Esther; it is the inspiring story of a beautiful woman whose courage and honor saved her entire people from destruction. When you read it, compare the differing personalities of Queen Esther and her predecessor, Vashti. They both became queens because of their beauty, but Vashti forfeited her crown because of her attitude toward her husband, which in turn, was a reflection of her personality. She was unwilling to compromise or to humor him, and in so doing, she managed to turn an insignificant request into a conflict with him that cost her both her husband and her position as queen. The two prominent personality traits she displayed were willfulness and stubbornness, neither of which served her well. She was, instead, a prime example of the truth of Proverbs 14:1: "The wise woman builds her house, but the foolish pulls it down with her hands."

There are many other women in the Bible whose stories provide us with examples of both good and bad personality traits. Even if their attributes are not spelled out by name, their actions and attitudes provide ample evidence of their inner beauty, or lack thereof. Compare Sarah and Naomi to Jezebel and Delilah. Take a close look at Ruth, Mary, and Rahab, or Bathsheba, Herodias, and Salome. Hannah,

Deborah, Abigail—the lives of all of these women and dozens of others are outlined in the Old and New Testaments.

The Bible does not attempt to gloss over or sanitize the images of the men and women who inhabit its pages. They are people with strengths, weaknesses, lusts, good and bad actions, and characteristics, all intact. They are actual human beings, not saints and not monsters, just people. And as such, their character traits and actions that were pleasing to God are also accessible to us, if we take care to cultivate them in our lives.

As these verses point out, inner beauty in a woman is even more crucial than physical beauty to her overall attractiveness. That beauty of spirit is what counts most when your goal is to keep a man. Your appearance may initially attract his interest, but your personality and the manifestation of the fruit of the Spirit in you is what will make him want to stay by your side. As you work on your outward appearance don't neglect to do an honest appraisal of your personality. You probably already have a pretty clear idea of areas that could use some improvement, but don't accept the common excuse, "That's just the way I am," as a reason for not even attempting to change.

TEMPERAMENT AND YOU

If you've never studied about temperaments and their corresponding personality traits, I strongly recommend that you read *Spirit Controlled Temperament* by Christian psychologists Tim and Beverly LaHaye, or *Personality Plus* by Florence Littauer. In these and other books, authors have outlined the basic personality groups that God has created and the subgroup combinations possible among them. You'll no doubt be surprised to recognize yourself in one or more of them. When you get over your surprise that they have done such a good job of describing you, you'll begin to better understand and accept yourself. You'll find that many of the characteristics and reactions that you may have felt were strange, unique to you, or just plain weird about you, are actually commonplace and quite normal for your personality type. An understanding of temperament is also very useful in accepting and coping with the traits and tendencies of other people in your life. In addition, you'll begin to understand how God can work in your life to change, modify, or compensate for the less desirable aspects of your personality.

Try to secure a copy of these or other temperament studies at your local Christian bookstore. Recognizing yourself and understanding the personality traits of all the temperament groups is both fun and informative.

THE GOD-CENTERED PERSONALITY

No matter what your temperament type, or combination thereof, God is what makes the difference. Even though you possess certain inherent personality traits, God can help you modify their manifestation. For instance, if you are prone to impatience and explosive outbursts of anger, God can give you the means for self-control, if you pray and seek His help. Be careful, however, before you ask Him for patience. He has some very effective but extremely trying methods of developing that particular fruit in your life. I know because I asked once, and almost instantly most everything in my life became a trial requiring patience.

The key to building your inner beauty is to consciously seek the fruit of the Spirit in your life first. The manifestation of this fruit will then begin to develop naturally if you are a God-centered woman who earnestly seeks to please Him. You will first consciously learn to control your tongue, to refrain from gossip, or speaking evil of others. Then you will automatically begin to do so. Choose Jesus as your role model; stop and think about Him, and what His reaction to a situation would be, then ask a quick prayer for guidance and act accordingly. Of course, you'll not always succeed in doing the right thing, but you'll be learning and practicing, and beginning to acquire the habit of thinking like Him. Others will begin to see Jesus in you, and there is no greater beauty for any Christian, man or woman.

Part 3

HIM, NOT YOU

"For the ways of man are before the eyes of the LORD, and He ponders all his paths."

Proverbs 5:21

Introduction

Understanding the Christian Male Mind-Set

For most Single Christian Women (SCW) a list of interests in order of priority would read: God, myself, Single Christian Man/Men (SCM). (Note: in this section of the book, we're going to use these designations simply because they'll come up so often you'll get as tired reading the words as I will writing them.)

It is due primarily to lack of exposure that many SCW fail to truly understand how the minds of SCM work, and the ways in which they differ from the men they knew before they became Christians. There is a big difference. Of course, we all realize that each man is unique and a lot depends upon how deeply developed a man's relationship with God is.

Still, there are some basic tenets, applying to Christian men, married or single, that are as fundamental to their natures as is their maleness itself. It's important that you, as an interested female, become familiar with these basics. Part of your readiness to receive such a SCM as a mate, with whom you propose to live reasonably happily ever after, depends upon your knowledge of, understanding of, and acceptance of his nature as a Christian. It's not really such a hard job. Most everything about him and his mind-set is clearly spelled out in the pages of the Bible. In the next few chapters, which are devoted to understanding SCM, we'll explore many of

God's fundamental guidelines for the Christian man, in order to:

- help you understand basic Christian male orientation.
- help you discern the presence of God in the life of the men you meet.
- help you to accept and understand the ways in which you and he may differ, and possibly even clash.

Until this point our focus has been on you—on getting you in tune with God's plan, and on the action steps available to you while you await God's answer to your prayers. The third and equally vital phase for preparing you to receive your mate involves coming to terms with and learning to deal with men in their reality, as opposed to a self-centered dream of the perfect prince. As you probably long ago discovered, despite the claims of feminists to the contrary, men and women really do view and react to life from fundamentally divergent perspectives. Yet, with a little tolerance and a lot of acceptance, we can learn not only to accommodate our differences but to actually value them as being God-ordained. As women we can adjust to the task of peacefully functioning as a member of a couple by learning more about His male creation, then striving to "let go and let God."

Chapter 12

What Does He Want?

What a complicated question, asked daily by thousands of women who subconsciously feel that if they could only be sure of the answer, they could somehow transform themselves to conform to that answer and thereby be assured of finding and keeping a mate forever. It should all be so simple, but it isn't.

In order to understand what the SCM wants we must first clarify what he is. There are biblical fundamentals that delineate the male mentality; Scriptures that form the bedrock beliefs of most Christian men, regardless of denominational trappings and regardless of any references to women made by the Bible in the same context. I have purposely omitted the Bible's inclusion of women in listing these verses, because the objective here is to outline the Word as Christian men commonly view its references to them. Remember, this is not about you. It's about him.

WHAT IS HE?

1. He Is Created in God's Own Image

- Genesis 1:26. "Then God said, 'Let Us make man in Our image, according to Our likeness.'"
- Genesis 1:27. "So God created man in His own image; in the image of God He created him."

2. He Is Given to Ruling

- Genesis 1:26. "Let them have dominion over the fish of the sea, over the birds of the air, and over the cattle, over all the earth and over every creeping thing that creeps on the earth."
- Genesis 1:28. "Have dominion over the fish of the sea, over the birds of the air, and over every living thing that moves on the earth."

3. He Is Head Over the Woman, and Answers to Christ in the Chain of Command

- Genesis 3:16. "Your desire shall be for your husband, and he shall rule over you."
- 1 Corinthians 11:3. "But I want you to know that the head of every man is Christ, the head of woman is man, and the head of Christ is God."
- 1 Peter 3:1. "Wives, likewise, be submissive to your own husbands."
- Ephesians 5:22. "Wives, submit to your own husbands, as to the Lord."
- Ephesians 5:23. "For the husband is head of the wife, as also Christ is head of the church."
- Ephesians 5:33. "Let the wife see that she respects her husband."

4. He Has Rule Over His House

- 1 Timothy 3:12. "Let deacons be the husbands of one wife, ruling their children and their own houses well."
- Genesis 18:19. "He may command his children and his household after him."
- 1 Timothy 3:5. "For if a man does not know how to rule his own house, how will he take care of the church of God?"

5. His Primary Role Is to Work to Provide for His Household

- Genesis 3:17. "Cursed is the ground for your sake; in toil you shall eat of it all the days of your life."

- Genesis 3:19. "In the sweat of your face you shall eat bread."
- Exodus 20:9. "Six days you shall labor and do all your work."

6. He Is the Priest for His Family
- Joshua 24:15. "But as for me and my house, we will serve the LORD."
- Deuteronomy 32:46. "Set your hearts on all the words which I testify among you today, which you shall command your children to be careful to observe—all the words of this law."

7. He Is Head of the Church
- 1 Corinthians 14:34. "Let your women keep silent in the churches."
- Acts 6:3. "Therefore, brethren, seek out from among you seven men of good reputation, full of the Holy Spirit and wisdom, whom we may appoint over this business."
- Acts 14:23. "So when they had appointed elders in every church, and prayed with fasting, they commended them to the Lord in whom they had believed."

Most Christian men have no trouble understanding and accepting these aspects of their roles as men. They tend to feel that these rules are so clear that there should be no confusion or discussion of them with the women in their lives. If you, however, have a problem accepting men in these roles, or with relinquishing your own control in these areas, you must make an extra effort to find out what God is truly saying.

TESTIMONY TIME
In case you do struggle with any of the precepts outlined here, please don't feel that you are alone. As I noted earlier, one of the biggest adjustments I faced after accepting Jesus Christ as Lord of my life was to lift my hands and my mind from their tight control over my life. My attitude was that I

had done a commendable job of raising my kids alone and running my life for many years. Why then should I now allow a man to become lord over me? I was answerable to no one but God Himself.

Every time the pastor preached a sermon on the roles of men and women in marriage, all of my old worldly beliefs reared their heads. Didn't he know that times had changed? Didn't he know that I worked five days a week, drew a full paycheck, and spent it as I pleased? What about the rights of women? I could handle submitting myself to God, but voluntarily giving way to a man went against my grain in a big way.

What I had never stopped to consider was the degree and effectiveness of the indoctrination that the world had put into my life. It never occurred to me that this conviction of mine might be diametrically opposed to biblical principles, as are most of the ways of the world.

Fortunately, I was in a church that was so deeply rooted in biblical teachings that I had the opportunity to advance beyond primary, spoon-fed Christianity to a greater level of biblical scholarship. The church offered in-depth Bible classes with skilled teachers. Additionally, we were constantly encouraged to read the Bible and study it for ourselves.

Unless you read the Word for yourself, however, you have no choice but to accept its interpretation as presented to you by someone else. Even though it is essential that we hear and follow the preachings and teachings of a pastor, it is even more essential that we study the Bible itself and allow God to speak to us through His Holy Spirit. As my study of the Bible intensified I found myself taking issue with the Word itself more and more. When I began to question the Word of God with God Himself, I found that I had no grounds whatsoever on which to stand. There is no gray area in God's Bible. There is only the truth of the Word. You either accept it and grow to understand His Word, or you place yourself in rebellion to it. You must decide for yourself.

ARE YOU REALLY READY?

The drastic modification of this "rights" attitude was one of the most essential changes God wrought in me to prepare me for the delivery of my mate. He opened my eyes to the realization that submission to a husband would provide me with a place of shelter and safety I had never experienced before. Contrary to diminishing me, it would give me the security to attempt new things and to change and grow under a God-ordained umbrella of protection.

Of course, each relationship is different, and the spouses involved must come to terms with whatever accommodations might be required within their own household. Frequently, they decide to allocate to one person primary control over one aspect of the home, and to the other, control in another area. Such compromises are not the issue; each couple is free to develop their own internal marital structure. God's concern is, however, that there be no debate over who is responsible for the house—He looks to the man as the designated overseer.

It is vital that you come to terms with the roles outlined here, and be very clear about your ability to tolerate them, before you marry. If you're not ready to deal with such restrictions, perhaps those mating prayers are somewhat premature. You need to, through prayer and working it out with God, determine your own readiness and willingness to actually welcome the role of being married to a Christian man. If you will function more as a hindrance than a help in the life of the man you desire, you can rest assured that God will take you out of his life. So before you commit, be prepared to submit.

A note of caution here: Don't take the submission concept to an extreme and think that the Bible requires you to submit to almost any person just because he is a man. If the guy is not your husband, how you respond to him is up to you.

Chapter 13

What Should He Be?

The wisdom of the Bible is all-inclusive. There is virtually no subject of concern to the Christian that is not addressed within its pages, either directly or indirectly. For you, as a SCW, it contains a wealth of advice on what constitutes the characteristics of a good man, and therefore, a good mate. Throughout its chapters we are given not only illustrations of the lives of good men, but specific descriptive verses on their attributes, as well. We need to consider these Scriptures because, as with everything in it, the wisdom of the Word is absolute truth, and you ignore or disregard it only to your own detriment.

CLUES/DESCRIPTIONS

There are several major areas of concern that God addresses regarding a man's basic personality traits. It is essential that you pay close attention to how the men in your life respond in these areas:

Anger
- Proverbs 22:24. "Make no friendship with an angry man, and with a furious man do not go."
- Proverbs 29:22. "An angry man stirs up strife, and a furious man abounds in transgression."

- Proverbs 14:17. "A quick-tempered man acts foolishly, and a man of wicked intentions is hated."
- Proverbs 15:18. "A wrathful man stirs up strife, but he who is slow to anger allays contention."
- Proverbs 16:32. "He who is slow to anger is better than the mighty, and he who rules his spirit than he who takes a city."

Laziness

- Proverbs 14:23. "In all labor there is profit, but idle chatter leads only to poverty."
- Proverbs 24:33–34. "A little sleep, a little slumber, a little folding of the hands to rest; so shall your poverty come like a prowler, and your need like an armed man."
- Proverbs 19:15. "Laziness casts one into a deep sleep, and an idle person will suffer hunger."
- Ecclesiastes 10:18. "Because of laziness the building decays, and through idleness of hands the house leaks."

Self-Control

- Proverbs 25:28. "Whoever has no rule over his own spirit is like a city broken down, without walls."
- Ecclesiastes 7:8. "The patient in spirit is better than the proud in spirit."
- Colossians 3:8. "But now you yourselves are to put off all these: anger, wrath, malice, blasphemy, filthy language out of your mouth."

Foolishness

- Proverbs 14:7. "Go from the presence of a foolish man, when you do not perceive in him the lips of knowledge."
- Proverbs 12:15. "The way of a fool is right in his own eyes, but he who heeds counsel is wise."
- Proverbs 19:1. "Better is the poor who walks in his integrity than one who is perverse in his lips, and is a fool."
- Proverbs 18:7. "A fool's mouth is his destruction, and his lips are the snare of his soul."

Wisdom

- Ecclesiastes 8:1. "Who is like a wise man? And who knows the interpretation of a thing? A man's wisdom makes his face shine, and the sternness of his face is changed."
- Proverbs 13:15. "Good understanding gains favor, but the way of the unfaithful is hard."
- Proverbs 14:16. "A wise man fears and departs from evil, but a fool rages and is self-confident."
- Ecclesiastes 10:12. "The words of a wise man's mouth are gracious, but the lips of a fool shall swallow him up."
- James 3:13. "Who is wise and understanding among you? Let him show by good conduct that his works are done in the meekness of wisdom."
- James 3:17. "But the wisdom that is from above is first pure, then peaceable, gentle, willing to yield, full of mercy and good fruits, without partiality and without hypocrisy."

Honesty

- Proverbs 12:17. "He who speaks truth declares righteousness, but a false witness, deceit."
- Proverbs 13:5. "A righteous man hates lying, but a wicked man is loathsome and comes to shame."
- Proverbs 12:22. "Lying lips are an abomination to the LORD, but those who deal truthfully are His delight."

Goodness

- Micah 6:8. "He has shown you, O man, what is good; and what does the LORD require of you but to do justly, to love mercy, and to walk humbly with your God?"
- Proverbs 13:6. "Righteousness guards him whose way is blameless."
- Proverbs 13:9. "The light of the righteous rejoices, but the lamp of the wicked will be put out."
- Proverbs 13:21. "Evil pursues sinners, but to the righteous, good shall be repaid."

These are just a few of the descriptions of manly virtues put forth in the Bible mostly from the book of Proverbs. Use these verses; store them in your mind as criteria to employ in the evaluation of a man's potential as a mate. They serve as guidelines for a man to pattern his behavior by and as guides for a woman on what to look for. The world may tell you to seek riches, or looks, or education in your choice of a mate, but the Lord tells you to search his character instead, for that is the true evaluation of his manhood and a sure indication of what it will be like to live with him.

According to the Bible, a good, kind, wise man, with an even temper is a man of great worth, but a fool will be a constant source of trial to you, his wife. The story of Abigail (see 1 Samuel 25) provides an excellent illustration of this truth. The Bible says she was "a woman of good understanding and beautiful appearance; but the man was harsh and evil in his doings" (1 Sam. 25:3). After he foolishly insulted King David, she found herself hastening down the road to head off David's attack against her husband, herself, and their entire household. Only by her quick intervention were their lives spared. Abigail could have paid an extremely high price for having married a fool.

One other crucial character trait you must consider in a mate is purity. Refer back to chapter 3 and our discussion of fornication and adultery for a listing of pertinent Scriptures, and bear in mind that these verses are just as applicable to the man as they are to you. Your mate must not be a whoremonger, a man given to random fornication or adultery, but must instead have gained dominion over bodily lusts and desires. Hebrews 13:4 states that "Marriage is honorable among all, and the bed undefiled; but fornicators and adulterers God will judge." Very few women have the fortitude to tolerate a husband who is continually given to committing adultery and God does not require you to. Adultery is virtually the only reason that He considers divorce permissible, and you would be wise to carefully consider indications of the presence of this characteristic in the lives of the men you date. In this age of lethal sexually transmitted diseases, the decision to marry a man given to sexual immorality could have life or death implications.

We won't even attempt to address here the difficulties of living with a man who suffers under the bondage of addictions. Drugs and alcohol wreak havoc even among Christians, particularly in those who have been converted while yet under their control. They must continually fight Satan to keep him from regaining lost ground and seizing control of their actions once again. It is an arduous task, requiring extraordinary vigilance and commitment on the part of both husband and wife.

Rather than disregard warning signs of impending trouble in the men you date, you must keep your eyes open and proceed cautiously. Diligently seek God's direction for the gift of a good man, one who, according to Isaiah 33:15, "walks righteously and speaks uprightly, he who despises the gain of oppressions, who gestures with his hands, refusing bribes, who stops his ears from hearing of bloodshed, and shuts his eyes from seeing evil." Read all of Psalm 112 for a further description of the virtues you should seek in the man you marry, and study 2 Timothy 3 in its entirety for a vivid description of what you should avoid. First Timothy 6:11 follows up with the admonition, "But you, O man of God, flee these things and pursue righteousness, godliness, faith, love, patience, gentleness."

Lastly, give ear to what your own spirit tells you about the character of the man you desire. There will be plenty of clues available to show you what he is really like, and the Holy Spirit will quicken your awareness of them, if you will only listen to your own inner voice. If you and the Lord stay in close touch with each other, He will not let you blunder foolishly ahead without attempting to guide you away from trouble. As usual, you've got to trust Him and pray.

Chapter 14

Well, Isn't He?

Since you are heeding the biblical admonition to marry a Christian, perhaps you have begun to wonder how your Christian mate could be anything other than the paragon of virtue described in the verses that illustrate the qualities of a good man. Surely he will have none of the negative contrasts with which God ends almost all of these verses. You can be assured that if your friend is truly a Christian, you have the best possible start, for only with a Christian man can you have a Christian marriage, ordained, sanctified, and guided by God Himself.

Still, this is a man who was born and raised in the world, and probably lived by its codes for a long time before he truly committed his life to Christ. His temperament and personality traits were fully formed in the world, and though the Lord may have wrought a tremendous work or even a miraculous change in his life, he is still under construction. Many of the old ways and habits that he struggled against in the past may still remain under certain conditions, and they will likely continue to do so. Negative traits are particularly prone to reappear in stressful situations or during periods of trial, and thus may often recur until many years of walking with God have eased them into the background. When he reaches a point of Christian maturity, the Lord will have achieved primary control in his life, and the man will have learned to consistently ward off any attempts of his old self to rear its ugly head. Until he arrives at that transformed state, however, both you and he may still have to confront remnants of the old man.

You are correct if you believe that God can change a person. You are also correct if you feel that the presence of God in your man's life can overcome any flaws that may reveal themselves. God equips and enables us to defeat the devil even as manifested in our own personalities. He does indeed work all things out to His glory and honor. His glory is truly revealed whenever He exhibits His patient work over time, by transforming an ordinary SCM into the man of God He has ordained him to be.

When I advised caution in the last chapter, in evaluating the character of your potential mate, it was with the implied understanding that you have sought Jesus Christ first on this matter . . . that you have checked yourself for any tendencies toward unrealistic expectations, and that you are not fully committed to holding out for the arrival of a fantasy man but instead are receptive to God's will. If you can indeed deal with the foibles of a real man, that's exactly what God will give you. You may even have been especially prepared for this mate, designed with the innate capacity to tolerate his specific imperfections. If that is so, you need only pray that the Lord will grant you the strength to see the task through, to reach that glorious point when your husband has been completely renewed through God's patient work in his life, and His love abounding in you.

However, unless God has specially gifted you to minister to a man in his area of weakness, you would be well advised to heed the character admonitions detailed in the last chapter.

Check your motives. What's the lure? Maybe he has some overwhelming redeeming quality that you find irresistible. Or is he just unbelievably handsome, or so incredibly stimulating that you've taken leave of your senses? Perhaps you've decided to make him your own personal mission field. Or are you in search of a heavy burden, some sort of affliction or cross to bear, in order to satisfy a latent martyr complex? Are you wearing permanently affixed rose-colored glasses that refuse to acknowledge his faults? Or are you just desperate to marry? These are all very poor foundations on which to build a marriage.

The point to remember is that you should want from God His very best in a mate. Of course, it is possible to be a Christian, even a strong Christian, and still be seriously flawed; and as we have stated before, it is well within God's abilities to correct any such character problems. But can you successfully live with this man while you wait it out? Not all transformations occur overnight. In fact, most require months or years of patience, tolerance, and long-suffering. Be careful what you ask for; you may get it.

ONE MORE THING

There is one final characteristic we have not yet considered that is of extreme importance to you. It is possible to love and to live peaceably with almost any Christian man, regardless of overt flaws, as long as he obeys God's admonition to love you, his wife. God has commanded that a husband love his wife. A woman who is truly loved can put up with almost any imperfection. Some Scriptures that help us to understand the love a husband should have for his wife include:

- Colossians 3:19. "Husbands, love your wives and do not be bitter toward them."
- Ephesians 5:28. "So husbands ought to love their own wives as their own bodies; he who loves his wife loves himself."
- Ecclesiastes 9:9. "Live joyfully with the wife whom you love all the days of your vain life."
- Ephesians 5:25. "Husbands, love your wives, just as Christ also loved the church and gave Himself for her."

The man who truly cares for and loves his wife as Christ loved us and continues to love the church has an automatic check on his destructive tendencies and hurtful actions. It is a large task that God has called him to. Jesus loves the church sacrificially, and willingly gave His own life for it. He also loves it unconditionally; not providing or withholding His love arbitrarily, predicated upon its actions, but loving no matter what. He acts always for the good of the church and meets its every need. In the book of Revelation, the church, the body of believers, is characterized as the Bride of Christ, those He has selected above all others to be united with Him forever.

When a SCM selects his wife, he makes an equally binding and irrevocable commitment. If he sincerely adheres to God's Word and strives to truly love his wife in an openly affectionate manner, she, in turn, will find herself almost automatically willing to submit to him and to please him. She will discover that she is happily giving to him parts of herself that she would not normally be inclined to surrender. His strivings to love his wife will not immediately overcome the negative aspects of his personality, but they will serve as a check on his actions, a reference point to make him stop and think before he heads off too far down the wrong road. Causing hurt, pain, or disappointment to a wife does not conform to the injunction to love her.

A man who works hard to honor his obligations as a Christian husband is a godly man, one to be treasured by his wife. This is yet another persuasive argument for limiting your selection of a mate to those who are within the Christian fold. A non-Christian man has no such check on his spirit. He feels he is free to do as he pleases, and will often do so, to the detriment of his wife and family. The constraints of God are an irrelevant issue to him; therefore, there can be no benefits from serving God in his life that will accrue to you, his wife. But your Christian mate will seek to please God and almost by default will also please you.

So, don't arbitrarily discount a SCM for his faults. Rather, be sure that you follow God's admonitions, and that the flaws in your intended mate are such that you can live with them, work with them, and seek to modify them within the confines of both the will of your man and the will of God. You cannot change him by your efforts alone. In fact, it is best that you simply accept them and not seek to change him at all, at least in an overt manner. Instead, rely upon God through prayer to bring him into conformity to God's will.

Pray, pray, pray. And realize that if you and your man love each other and love God, there is no problem too great to be solved; "All things are possible with God," and even your seriously flawed mate can grow to be a living testimony to the saving grace of Jesus Christ. Is he worth taking the risk? Only you can decide.

Chapter 15

What Does He Need?

Aside from what he is and how he acts, there is yet another issue to consider. What does he, as a SCM, actually need and require from the woman whom God gives to him? Yes, he does have needs; there are psychological requirements that he can derive only from his wife. The old criteria of hot meals, clean clothing, and a satisfying sex life are not the issues to be addressed here. Rather, we are concerned with the deep-seated, innermost necessities demanded by his masculinity, that only you, as his feminine counterpart, can provide. Yes, Mr. Tough, Mr. Strong, Mr. Invincible is dependent upon you, to validate him and to supply a surprising number of needs in his manly life. And he will gravitate unswervingly to the woman who is able to supply them. Let's discuss what men need.

1. RESPECT

This is a man's most vital psychological need, rivaling even sex in overall importance. The dictionary defines respect as follows: "to feel or show honor or esteem for; hold in high regard; to consider or treat with deference or dutiful regard." Ephesians 5:33 enjoins wives to "respect" their husbands. First Peter 3:1–6 discusses how even a non-Christian man can be won over by observing a wife's "chaste conduct accompanied by fear," and how "Sarah obeyed

Abraham, calling him lord." In the story of David, his wife, Michal, is put away from the king for despising him in her heart (see 2 Sam. 6:16–23); and in Esther 1:9–12, the imprudent Vashti, whom we discussed in an earlier chapter, lost her crown for refusing to obey her husband. On the other hand, the diligent, ever energetic, paragon of virtue in Proverbs 31, "did her husband good" always, as he sat among the respected elders at the gate, and she thus reaped the honor of eternal praise for her many virtues.

Read your Bible. Nowhere in it is the wife commanded to love her husband. She is, instead, told to respect and obey him. Only the man is instructed to love.

As with many things in life, we most often value and seek out that which is hard to get. A man often feels that a woman who will love him can be easily found but one who will respect and honor him as a man is a rarity, especially in today's society, which has been so influenced by the feminist movement. Many women, on the other hand, don't care nearly as much about what a man can give them as they do about how he treats them. His concern for her feelings, complete with understanding hugs and kisses, and his commitment to forsake all others are more important to her happiness than the size of the diamond on her engagement ring or how much money is stored in the bank for their retirement.

Never the twain shall meet? Not so. God intended the natural traits of men and women to balance and complement each other. One is strong in the area where the other is weak. Amazingly enough, it tends to work out just as God planned. A wife gains respect for a husband who loves her, and a man grows to love the wife who respects him.

Though it may not come naturally to you, respect can become a habit by your actions. Before you nag, debate, or ridicule your man's suggestion or request, stop for a moment. Does his proposal merit the scorn you are preparing to heap upon it?

2. TO LEAD

The spirit of competition is useful in some areas of life, but when it pits you against your husband in a struggle for supremacy, it is destructive. What follows is what the Lord has given me. I don't profess to have totally attained what I am about to say but I'm striving. I know how I should think and act in this area, but acquiescing continues to be an on-going task, though not insurmountable.

In the last chapter we looked at numerous verses where God assigns to the man a leadership role, actually even a leadership burden. Leadership means headship and control, and most men strive for it quite naturally, not only in leadership over their women and families, but also among each other. They tend to expect and even enjoy the leadership struggle among themselves, but most of them greatly resent having to struggle for authority with the woman they love. A wise woman understands this male ego demand, and grants her husband or boyfriend this right.

Because you, God's precious SCW pearl, are not yet yoked to a man, you may not often struggle with this concept in the abstract, but it is best that you try to come to terms with it now, before God grants your prayer request. While I was dating and waiting, the concept seemed much simpler. Depending upon my mood, I was not only willing, but eager to hand myself over. "Here I am. Here's my life. Someone run it." Yet, when faced with the reality of accepting a man's dominance, many women, myself included, struggle with the actuality, often because they subconsciously lack trust in their man's leadership capabilities. This is the real reason for much of the nagging that so many women resort to when they do get married; the nagging that tends to drive most men somewhat crazy. Proverbs 21:9 declares that it is "better to dwell in a corner of a housetop, than in a house shared with a contentious woman." Proverbs 27:15 notes that "a continual dripping on a very rainy day and a contentious woman are alike."

You know how you would handle a given situation—God forbid that your man's idea should prove to be different. But he doesn't think like you, and that is probably one of his greatest strengths. Rather than contesting him on every decision and enduring the bickering and strife that invariably follow, try prayer instead. Pray to God to guide his decisions, and in your actions, yield to them.

Bear in mind, however, that true leadership implies benevolence of purpose; it means that the person leading has in mind the best interests of those whom God has given him the care of. This is where the "burden" comes about. A true leader (the only kind God calls) functions more as a servant than a master. He has been authorized by God to see to it that his charges arrive at the best, most beneficial place for them to possibly be. This responsibility is a tall order; not one to be assumed or treated lightly. When you, as a woman, subside and let your man accede to the leadership position, you have, by your actions, given him a vote of confidence and a crucial ego boost. He may immediately turn around and request your input or suggestions, but seeking counsel is his prerogative as the leader. In fact, Proverbs 19:20 declares that a man should "listen to counsel and receive instruction, that you may be wise in your latter days." That is not an admission of weakness, but rather, a gesture of strength on his part, and also, in these days, a wise move for keeping peace in his family.

3. TO PROVIDE

In his role as head of the household, God requires the man to provide for the material needs of his family. On a psychological level, men need to fulfill that role. If a man is mentally and physically healthy, his ego requires that he provide the material needs for his family. Most men provide for their families by working, and the topic of gainful employment is definitely addressed within the pages of the Bible:

- Proverbs 12:11. "He who tills his land will be satisfied with bread."
- Romans 12:10–11. "Be kindly affectionate to one another with brotherly love . . . not lagging in diligence, fervent in spirit, serving the Lord."
- Proverbs 22:29. "Do you see a man who excels in his work? He will stand before kings; he will not stand before unknown men."
- Ecclesiastes 5:3. "For a dream comes through much activity."
- Ecclesiastes 9:10. "Whatever your hand finds to do, do it with your might."
- Proverbs 18:9. "He who is slothful in his work is a brother to him who is a great destroyer."

Our wise God knew that giving the man the responsibility to provide for his loved ones would automatically make man more caring and concerned about others, as well as strengthen and weld the family unit together. On the other hand, Proverbs 19:24 states, "A lazy man buries his hand in the bowl, and will not so much as bring it to his mouth again." In other words, this poor specimen of manhood would rather starve than work, and he's definitely not interested in sharing or meeting the needs of others. He is unfit for marriage unless the Lord changes him.

THE PROBLEM

Few women are reluctant to grant their men the responsibility of providing. It is rarely a contested issue, but this requirement often becomes problematic for many men, even the ones with the best intentions. For example, a man faces a great deal of stress, if, due to economic or educational limitations, he finds himself unable to find a job that pays enough to adequately support his family. Also, as a matter of course, if he is mentally unstable, addicted, or just plain lazy, both he and his family will suffer physical and emotional hardship.

However, in our American society, most men face the additional challenge presented by a working wife. In God's original plan the woman tended the home and the kids while the man farmed, hunted, engaged in commerce, or did whatever else he needed to do to keep his household fed, sheltered, and clothed. Most men today do not have the slightest objection to their wives working, nor do the wives wish to while away hours at home, unless they are attempting to raise small children. Often, the cost of living does not permit the woman the option to stay at home. However, it is crucial that this not become an issue between the mates. A wife with superior earning capability must not succumb to the temptation to seize control or to belittle her husband, while a man must not feel diminished because of his wife's contributions to their support. The detrimental effects of either of these attitudes can undermine the entire structure of the relationship. The same is true if a woman wants to stay home and rear her children but is forced to work out of economic necessity; or if her husband opposes her job but has no choice but to live with it. These types of resentments must not be permitted to arise between the partners. The two are one, and in their unity is their strength.

Money. The love of, the lack of, or the distribution thereof, is the single most prevalent source of conflict in most marital relationships. It need not become a divisive factor in your upcoming marriage, if you learn now, that the ability to provide for you and for his family is crucial to your man's self-esteem. Never deride his efforts to earn an income. Instead, encourage him to keep trying hard to be the best at whatever he does. God will reward him for it. No matter what his job, as long as it is legal and not contrary to God's will, if he is consistently and persistently good at it, the Lord Himself will bring promotion. Psalm 75:6–7 says, "For exaltation comes neither from the east nor from the west nor from the south. But God is the Judge: He puts down one, and exalts another." Diligence and hard work, coupled with prudence and a godly spirit, can bring prosperity to any man. Proverbs

14:23 says, "In all labor there is profit." Watch for this characteristic of diligence in the men you date. Whether he is a laborer or an executive, his attitude toward working is of vital importance. He must accept it as his God-given responsibility and approach it with enthusiasm and focus. You will both reap what he sows.

Unfortunately, many men bind their self-worth with their ability to provide for their wives. Thus, if the wife is well educated or highly paid, the man may no longer feel that he performs a vital function in the relationship. "Why does she need me? She can take care of herself better than I can," is a common lament of husbands in this predicament. Only the wife, by her actions and attitude, can provide the reassurance that he needs. The most effective way to let him know he is truly needed is by treating him with respect and deference and by letting him be the overseer of the household as God called him to be. Don't make the mistake of assuming that your love is enough. He can find love almost anywhere. Do what God instructs you to do, and be the woman who respects as well as loves her spouse and meets his emotional needs. It's an unbeatable combination.

In your current unmarried state, you probably regard this chapter as being a bit premature. However, one of the best ways that a single woman can prepare herself for eventual marriage is to make the effort to acquire an understanding of the mysterious and complicated male mind-set. You will often encounter this male mystique in dating situations. Prior to marriage, I decided that my understanding of Christian men was so inadequate that I enrolled myself in the married women's class at church. I figured it would be a great place to gain insight into how men think and it was. You'll find that the needs of men, as outlined here, are common to both married and single men, and your awareness of these characteristics will help to smooth what could be a rocky relationship, even before you marry.

Chapter 16

Getting Your Needs Met—Can He Do It?

The final area of concern that we need to address, regarding the man you may be praying about as your future mate, is his response to you and the special needs you have as a woman. God has mandated that he meet your basic needs. Unfortunately, this does not include your whims, fleeting desires, or fantasies. Sure, it might be nice if he could be tall, smart, and handsome; buy you a big nice house; and gratify your urge to "shop till you drop." However, these pleasant attributes are not enough to make you happy with him over the long haul because they don't reflect your true needs.

Before you recklessly declare that you have fallen in love with a man "regardless," take time for a long, hard, prayerful evaluation of how he reacts to you. Take off the rose-colored glasses and honestly consider what you really mean to him. Proverbs 19:14 says that "Houses and riches are an inheritance from fathers, but a prudent wife is from the LORD." Will he value and honor you as a wife? Does he even want one? Will he exalt you as his treasure or feel you are merely a trespass on his freedom? Whenever you hint at any sort of commitment, does he swing into a standard song of "don't fence me in," tell you how much he values his space, or go off on a tirade about his ex-wife?

Take a look at his male friendships. Does he have any? If not, why not? And, you must realize that if he's a chronic loner he may be prone to jealousy if you're the gregarious sort. If he does have friends, who are they? Are they committed Christian men or buddies from his former days before he was a Christian? Where do you fit in? Is it true that if you didn't shower him with phone calls, you wouldn't hear from him? Then there's a problem.

If your boyfriend or potential mate does not want and desire you, to the exclusion of almost everyone and anything else, he does not love you enough to begin a marital relationship. I feel you must be loved in excess at the outset, in order to be loved enough as the years go by. The intensity of love normally diminishes over time, and excess love simmers down to just enough love as the years pass and you become accustomed to each other. It is true that real love deepens and enriches as your shared life experience grows. But don't succumb to wishful thinking and try to wait and hope a nonexistent relationship into existence. It just won't happen.

What is your real position with the man you desire? Very often, women form close emotional bonds with men, based primarily upon friendship and conversation. They are usually dismayed that these friendships go nowhere, because in the man's mind, that is all they are. He may enjoy her company and like the fact that they can talk and share for hours; or appreciate being able to draw upon a feminine perspective. He may even be flattered by having a woman who cares for him or is obviously enthralled with him—it's a great ego booster, but most often it is not enough to make him commit to marriage.

There is another essential element that must first be present in men for a relationship to begin . . . true physical attraction, which is not simply about sex or lust, but has to do with being drawn to the actual physical presence of another person. It is this attraction that makes you special and different in his eyes from all other women.

It usually doesn't take a man forever to realize when that special attraction is there—in fact, some Christian psychologists and ministers feel that if a man hasn't decided to marry you after dating steadily for six months, he probably won't.

For the seriously marriage-minded SCW, an effective approach for developing a marriage-bound relationship is not to seek out a man she is attracted to and try to attract him to her, but rather, to choose her husband from among those special men to whom she is a treasure, a unique gift from God. I know it's hard, but no matter how infatuated you are, you must stay cool and calm in the early stages of a dating relationship, and let *him*, if he is so inclined, fall head over heels for you.

I believe that one of the most special moments in life is when the man you truly care for looks at you and the "eureka" light beams in his eyes. It's not a switch you can reach into his brain and snap on. In reality, the only way you can set it aglow is by standing back at enough distance from him so that he can clearly see you for the uniquely wonderful woman you are. Don't be afraid to give him space.

"NEED" AGAIN

A reminder of another fact that we noted earlier in this book; God will supply all your needs. When you truly need a husband, not just a sex partner or a friend, then He is faithful and prompt to supply all your needs. But your need, the sincere desire of your heart, must be there first. God answers prayers and meets needs; if you are fickle, unsure, or double-minded on the matter, He will wait, biding His time until you realize that you actually do need the husband you are praying for.

This is not a "Fatal Attraction" scenario. The need in your life for a husband must never be targeted as a need for a specific man. That attitude will only set you up for the obsessive round of unrequited desires outlined as Prophecy/Prediction Syndrome in chapter 4. Instead of targeting and trying to tackle a specific guy, leave that part up to the Lord. He already has the right man in mind for you. As a pastor friend of mine puts it, "Only God can put the right head with the right body." So let Him handle it.

ANSWERING THE CALL

Another situation I'm beginning to encounter with greater frequency among SCW that reflects our changing era and its attitude toward women, even among Christians, is that more and more SCW are beginning to recognize and respond to the call of God in various areas of Christian ministry. These include not only ministries of preaching and teaching but also ministering in special ways, such as functioning in the office of prophet or healer.

If you find that you have been called by God for a particular area of Christian ministry, you may also find that the presence of a husband could actually be a hindrance at this point in your life; and, if you are open to the call and the will of God, you will probably be able to abide by His schedule on the matter. In fact, if He does call you into Christian ministry, He will give you the ability to wait on Him for the appropriate time to marry. You shouldn't have to struggle greatly with this. On the other hand, you may be specially blessed to discover that you'll attract your future mate as a direct result of tending to your ministry, and that you would never have met him had you denied God's call.

As unequal as it may seem, after all the back and forth of courtship has been enacted, the man must be the one who wants you to share his life. You, however, are the only one who can decide if this is the man you should marry, the man who can uniquely respond to you as both a Christian and a woman. Don't settle for loving a man who brings you pain and suffering. Choose a man whose desire is to love you and bring joy into your life.

A word of caution is necessary before you trot off to live happily ever after. Never expect another person, even a husband, to "make you happy." Happiness is a transitory state. You can be pleased and happy with someone or something one minute and in no time at all be displeased or unhappy with the same person or thing. Every woman needs to understand this. No one, except you, is responsible for your personal happiness or lack thereof. The presence of Jesus Christ in your life brings joy, which is a constant state of your heart, regardless of circumstances or situations. But not even He guarantees happiness. So go ahead and choose the man who pleases you, with the understanding that joy is yours, but happiness is a blessing, not your right. Marriage does not come with that guarantee. Then go ahead and enjoy the kind of loving marriage that you truly desire, the one that God has ordained to meet your unique needs.

Part 4

TESTIMONIES

*"And they overcame him by
the blood of the Lamb and by
the word of their testimony."*

Revelation 12:11

Introduction

Testimony Time

As a Christian, you are already aware of the often spectacular way in which God works to bring about change in our lives. Even when you feel that your prayers are going unheeded and that God neither hears nor cares, the answers themselves are on the way. Recall for a moment the story in Daniel 10 where Daniel was told that as soon as he prayed God dispatched an angel with the answer. But the angel himself encountered resistance and was delayed by Satan in a battle designed to weaken Daniel's faith.

Don't think for one moment that this same struggle does not occur today. Have you been on your knees before God for what seems to be an unduly long season? Does it seem as if you are wasting your time, that your tears are being ignored . . . that God is responding only with silence?

I'm going to tell you a different story and so are the women whose testimonies you are about to read. As the introductory passage from Scripture indicates, the Christian's testimony is one of the most powerful weapons God has given us to overcome Satan. I've been excited about sharing these stories ever since God gave me the inspiration for this book. It was one of the very first things He showed me: the reality of His work in the everyday lives of Christians and how He answers prayers daily. Never ever give up on Him—if your faith is being tried, it is in order to strengthen you; if your commitment is being tested, it is so that you will emerge from the furnace as pure gold. You may waver and even doubt, but don't ever let Satan cause you to give up, and thus steal your victory away. You're God's precious pearl and He loves you. "He shall give you the desires of your heart" (Ps. 37:4).

The backgrounds of the women who have shared their testimonies here are varied. Two are former never-married singles, one of whom was previously a single mother. The others are survivors of divorces they neither wanted nor could control.

Enough said. Come, let me introduce you to . . .

BARBARA JACKSON

Age 51
Insight: It's Never Too Late

Barbara is a lovely, slender, youthful woman whose vitality makes her seem years younger. She is a talented singer who once traveled the world as the lead singer for the Ray Charles Raylettes. She is also a newlywed, having married Reverend Del Jackson a few months ago. Barbara dearly loves both the Lord and her new husband and was eager to share how, after many years as a single, God brought her the helpmate she had long desired.

JP: How did you and Del meet?

BJ: Del and I officially met in May of 1992 at my son-in-law's first church anniversary service. However, we'd met casually twice before, once the year before when he came to my son-in-law and daughter's house to pray for their first baby, then later at a neighbor's home Bible study. He seemed to be a very nice man, but beyond that I gave no thought to him at all, since he was married.

Then in February of 1992, his wife became ill and died on her birthday in March.

A couple of months later, I came down to Houston for my son-in-law's anniversary without realizing that Del was preaching the keynote sermon. I was happy to see him but I was going through a pretty rough period of depression at that time. I'd been crying for a week and simply had no one to turn to or to talk to. After the service I went up to Del and asked if he would pray for me whenever he got a chance. He did so right then. I instantly felt my burdens lift and we began chatting. I ended up issuing an open invitation for him and his daughter to come up to visit in Austin if they ever needed a change of scenery. He pressed me to name a date, so I told him Memorial Day. The next thing I knew, he was calling from a gas station, asking for directions. They had arrived a day early. I was running around in jeans, cleaning the house, and worrying frantically about how I would entertain this holy man. It turned out to be a great weekend, and about a month later we began dating. He proposed to me on the seventeenth of July.

JP: Did God work any miracles in bringing you together?

BJ: Definitely. God can change things in an instant. Del had been solidly married to one woman for twenty-three years, and I believe him when he says that he never played around or even flirted with other women. After she suddenly died, God healed his heart in a miraculous way before we ever even started talking. He made him ready for me.

In my own life, I had suffered a great deal of pain in my first marriage.

I realized later that God allowed me to go through all that hurt and suffering in order to prepare me.

JP: How long were you single? Did you ever give up hope of marrying again?

BJ: It's a funny thing. When I look back on it, God was already in the plan. He allowed me to be alone for twenty-one years. Sometimes my heart got very heavy. I met guys, even had several proposals, but I was fearful of putting my trust in anyone. Besides, the men I dated were not born-again, and I just wasn't willing to marry another non-Christian. Now I can really understand Romans 8:28, "All things work together for good to those who love God, to those who are the called according to His purpose."

Women think it's so hard to find a man that they'll settle for anything. After my divorce, I began to attend church regularly again, and through prayer and faith He held me together. God allowed me to rear my children alone—I was both mother and father, and yes, there were times I gave up hope of actually meeting Mr. Right. But, there was also a time span when I just wanted to get to know me. There were times when I asked the Lord to just make me content until He sent me someone; then there were other times when I asked, "Lord, what have I done, that I have not gotten what I asked for?"

Girlfriends offered me all kinds of advice. Fortunately, I've always had a strong mind; people couldn't convince or persuade me to do just anything.

Yes, I did give up hope sometimes. Even though I got proposals several times, I can only say, "Thank You, Lord," that I didn't get so desperate that I'd just take anything. I had to remind myself that if it's not of God, it's not going to work anyway; I'd have just ended up back in divorce court. There were many times when I cried at night, but I'm so glad I waited.

JP: Did God clue you in to your mate's arrival beforehand?

BJ: You know what the amazing thing is, He did. I had prayed for years, "Lord, send me a husband; Lord, send me a husband." In my later years I didn't want to be alone, and I didn't want to be wrapped up in my children. A girlfriend clued me in when she asked, "Have you ever thought about what you're saying? Do you know that a husband is a married man?" I'd never thought about it that way. God wants you to be specific to Him. I began to pray, "Lord, send me my helpmeet . . . the man whose rib You took me out of. Lord, You didn't place me here to be lonely; when You were lonely, You made man. You had to take me from somewhere—place me back there."

This was the positive prayer I prayed. Sure enough, there came a man I thought I loved before I met Del, but when you meet the real thing, you know the difference. It didn't take a man to meet my needs. It took the Lord Jesus Christ. I began to pick up my Bible and it was like food to me. I had been in the church my whole life. My daddy was a preacher and church was a part of me, but this was so different. I just didn't know how good God could be and what kind of joy He could bring. Psalm 34:8 says, "Oh, taste and see that the LORD is good." Well, His Word became food to me.

Even after that, though, sometimes I got weak in my spirit. Twenty-one years is a long time, and I sometimes questioned God. "Lord, when are You going to send me a man?" And when the despair would get to be too much, I would pray, "Lord, just take me away. My kids are grown now and I just don't want to go on alone." One night I was feeling so down that I went to the kitchen and made a little drink, a Coke and bourbon, even though I hardly ever drank. I crawled into bed with my drink and my Bible, in deep despair, but before I could take the first swallow, the phone rang. Out of nowhere, my friend Christopher Joy was on the phone and witnessed to me for two hours. What a blessing. The Lord came in right on time. He let me know that He'd heard my prayers and that the answer was on the way. After that, I knew my mate was coming, just not when; but in God's time.

JP: What kind of changes did the Lord have to make in you to prepare you for your husband?

BJ: You know, when I think about it, all that I went through prior to meeting him prepared me. You know you *do* have to have patience. God taught me that he wasn't going to come in my time but in His. I knew there were some things that God had to do in me and I actually started praying for those things to come to pass. I prayed, "Lord, do whatever it takes to shape me, straighten me, and make me right for my man, and make him right too, so that when we do come together, everything will be right with us," and that's just what He did.

He took me through some hard times and some good times, but through it all, He taught me that the power wasn't in me but in Him. I had to learn to depend on Him and not on myself. The power was in God's Holy Spirit. I know for certain that God wanted me to know Him before He allowed me to meet another man.

I learned that God wants to be first in your life; He's not going to be secondary to anyone. I went to church every

Sunday but I wasn't totally committed. He didn't move on my prayer until I came into total submission to Him. And we can't fool God. We can say, "Lord, I love You; Lord, I'll do this and that," but it means nothing because God knows just what we really mean. He knows when we are really ready.

I just thank Him. I never knew He was going to send me a preacher. I just asked Him for a man who really loved Him, because if he loved God, he'd know how to love me and everything else would fall into place. Respect, decency, all those things I wouldn't have to worry about if He gave me a man who truly loved Him.

JP: What would you like your overall testimony to others to be?

BJ: People see something different in me now. I am equally yoked and truly in love with a man in the way that God wants me to be. I do have a word of advice for women who are single mothers. First, you have to trust God and put Him first in your life. Second, live a decent life in front of your children. You can't be unholy and live an unholy life and expect your children to do right. You have to be honest and open with them. If you're a woman looking for a husband and you have problem children, not many men will want to deal with that. Who wants to buy into trouble? But if you have disciplined and respectful children, that makes a big difference. He'll come in and say, "Okay, these are nice, decent children, and so is their mother." You can't let your children rear you and expect someone else to come in and take over your problems. So, if you're a single woman with children, get your home right first.

If you're single with no children, my advice would be to always love God with all your heart, trust Him, wait on Him, seek Him, and pray an honest prayer. God truly knows your heart. If you're looking for self-pride, self-gratification, it won't work. You can't fool the Lord—He knows just what you need, and how much you need, and just when to show up on time. So you have to learn patience and totally trust the Lord. You can't ask and waver in faith. You have to ask in faith and believe.

Put your faith totally in God. Wait patiently on Him. Times may seem dark and it may seem like he's never going to show up, but if you ask in the Spirit, and believe truly in the Spirit without faltering faith, I can assure you God will deliver, and he'll come just when you least expect him. And when he comes, it'll be well worth the wait. We have to remember that "A thousand years is as one day with the Lord." What we call a long time is a short time to Him. He teaches us patience through all our tribulations, our heartaches, and our pain—He's there for us.

Start thanking God. Start praising Him for that helpmeet that He's going to send. Learn to thank Him in the midst of your tribulation. Your answer is on the way.

JP: Any admonitions or warnings to pass on?

BJ: Yes. The worse thing a person can do is to settle for a mate who does not love the Lord. God is so real and He makes it plain in His Word that He wants us equally yoked. He wants the very best for us, and if He wants the best for you, why should you settle for less? If you find a man who doesn't know Christ, no matter how much money he's got, how good he looks, or what kind of profession he's in, he's not worth losing your soul over. Don't waste your time.

And don't jump into bed with every man you meet. It's just not worth it—that's not going to show true love. Sex is not what love is all about because if you go to bed miserable, if you're drinking, you're on drugs, or whatever your trouble is, you're going to get up with that same problem you went to bed with, and more. That man's not going to solve them. He could be there for you today and gone tomorrow. But I can tell you with all my heart that God is there for you always. And He's there just when you need Him most. When you trust in Him and believe Him you can't be fooled by a love that's not real. When He sends your man He'll manifest Himself; He'll reveal Himself; He'll let you know there's something right about this relationship that's different from what you've ever experienced before.

WANDA ROBERSON

Age 37
Insight: A Woman of Integrity and Faith

Talking with Wanda is a remarkable experience. She is a petite and pretty woman, possessing the rare ability to present herself to others with total transparency and openness. It is due to the awe-inspiring movement of God in her life. She has been married to Pastor David O. Roberson of New Life Christian Center for approximately five months, and hers is one of the most inspiring testimonies I have yet encountered of how a marriage came to be.

JP: How did you and Dave meet?

WR: My church was having a guest minister over one Sunday night, a man who was a prophet. Our pastor told everybody to bring things we wanted to have prayed over and the prophet would pray about them. This guest minister was Pastor Gabriel Imoisi, David's best friend and brother in Christ, and David came along with him. During the service Pastor Gabriel called me out and began to prophesy that in April of the next year (this was October) the whole church would be rejoicing with me, and that my husband and I would never want or lack for anything, that we would be a family that served God, and on and on about me being married. In my mind I just shook my head and thought, "This man is missing God." Not only was I not married, I didn't even have the prospect of a date, and logic would tell you there was no way I'd be married in six months.

The object I had brought to be prayed over was the business proposal for the business God had promised me. That was the thing I was most interested in, and I laid this big, thick folder on the front of the altar among other people's wallets and handkerchiefs. When I went up to get it after the service, David came over and asked me what it was. He was very interested when I told him it was a business proposal and he kept asking me questions. He wanted to talk about investing and working on my financials, so I told him about a meeting coming up on Wednesday to review the proposal with backers. He asked for my phone number so he could call and be in prayer with me about it, and that was the only possible reason I would ever have given him my number. If he'd asked for any other reason, I would have said, "I think not," because I wasn't interested in anything else. I didn't know or care if he was married or single, or even if he had a wedding ring on. All I cared about was that he was interested in investing and praying about my business. On Monday night I got a call from him asking about the proposal, and we talked every day from then on.

God had already given me a personal conviction against dating. I was raising two young girls and I had no intention of parading men in and out of my house, trying this one out, trying that one out. I believed that "He who finds a wife finds a good thing," and that if it was for me, I'd know that this was the one when he found me. In the five years I had been single, I had dated only one guy. I went to the movies with him twice and that was the end of that. That was four years before and I hadn't been out since. When David asked me to go out to dinner with him, my reply was, "Sorry, but I don't date." So he asked me if he could set an appointment for a business lunch. That was fine with me, so we did. Then after two or three weeks he finally said, "Look, I'm not having any more appointments with you. We're dating." So that's how we ended up dating.

He now says that I'm the one who asked him to marry me, and I say he asked me. I guess it got confusing, because after three weeks of being on the phone, talking, and going out with each other, we both knew. You know how you can know something is from God but you're afraid to say it in case the other person isn't feeling the same way. So we were both very hesitant about saying we believed this was God's will for our lives. What we decided to do was to pray about it during his trip to Nigeria in December, and to use the separation to determine if we were hearing from God. When he came back we both felt the same way, but he was vacillating between, "Wanda, will you marry me?" and "I'm just not sure yet." He'd been single for eleven years and he needed to be certain. But I knew this was from God, and by the middle of January I got tired of that. So I drew up a contract that addressed seven specific issues, the first of which was: If he was serious about marriage I expected a date, time, and place to be set for our wedding. I signed it and told him I expected him to return it to me signed. He took it and looked at it with this look on his face that said, "She gave me a contract. I can't believe she gave me a contract."

He put it in a drawer and just wouldn't deal with it at all for a few days. But I told him that not signing it would end the relationship because I don't believe in just dating for the sake of dating. There has to be a purpose, a goal, or you leave the door open for the enemy to come in. I was not going to be in a relationship for a year or more and still not know where it was heading. I also wanted to know, as expressed in the contract, what the goals were for the marriage and for our family, and what his vision was for the church I would be marrying into.

He wouldn't tell me if he would sign or not, but he did really pray and seek the will of God about it. Then he told me he didn't need to sign. He knew that God had ordained me to be his wife. True to Pastor Gabriel's prophecy, we married in April after six months of courtship.

Later, God brought back to my remembrance a whole list of things I had asked for when I was really praying about marriage. I didn't want a long courtship—I wanted to meet and marry within six months, because I dated my first husband for six years and we were only married for eight, so a long courtship is no guarantee of longevity in marriage. I didn't want to go through that again. I also wanted to marry before my older daughter turned thirteen, because I wouldn't bring a man into the household with a teenage girl. Third, he had to love Christ more than he loved me. If he loved me more we'd have problems, because if he fell out of love with me, he'd have nothing to sustain him. But if he loved Jesus more, I wouldn't have to worry about him loving me. I also told God I wanted him to be a certain way, to look a certain way, and more, and every criterion I requested He granted.

JP: How did God prepare you for him?

WR: Well, I'd never met a man before with whom I was compatible in spirit, soul, and body. After my divorce, I realized that if I ever married again, my husband and I would have to be compatible in all three areas. Going through divorce was the hardest thing I'd ever been through in my life, and it literally pushed me into the arms of Jesus. I had no other options.

JP: Do you have any admonitions to pass on?

WR: Wait on God. Just wait on Him. It bothers me to see women who are not totally healed in their own emotions and not where they need to be in their relationship with God, yet they think a man is going to make them complete. They don't realize that no one can make you complete but Jesus. A man won't do it. One of the big mistakes I made in my first marriage was that I made my ex-husband responsible for my happiness. We have this Cinderella syndrome where we walk around looking for our Prince Charming, and think that when we meet him everything is going to be all right, our problems are going to be over. That's not true—our problems will just begin if we marry the wrong man. If I had not waited on God to do some things in me, some more perfecting, if I had stepped out on my own and tried to find a mate myself, I would have married wrong again, because I would have married for the wrong reasons.

I would say to anyone, search your motives before you get married. Are you getting married for the right reasons, or is 't because you're struggling financially, or you want a father for your kids, or you're just tired of being alone? Those are not good reasons to get married. Make sure you've heard the voice of God. Seek counsel. Get some godly counsel—go to your pastor since he's the watchman over your soul. Don't just operate out of what you want to believe. And remember, it's so easy for Satan to send a counterfeit because he knows exactly what we like. You've got to know God personally. Even with all this, we can make mistakes, but the chances become less likely the stronger our foundation is.

JP: Well, lastly, and having heard your testimony, I don't even have to ask, but what are your views on celibacy?

WR: Well, all I can say is that you can do it. God is well able to keep that which you commit to Him. My hardest time was when I was believing that my husband would come back and fighting that desire to be with my husband. After I'd gotten beyond that, after God had told me to let go of the marriage and stop fighting the divorce, God began to move in my life and I no longer desired him. The issue didn't come up again.

JP: What would you like your ultimate testimony to others to be?

WR: That I am a woman of integrity and faith in every area; that my word actually means something. It's just as important to walk in the fruit of the Spirit as it is to walk in the gifts of the Spirit because every tree must bear fruit. Your love, joy, peace, long-suffering, and character define and develop the person. Be fruitful and multiply.

BERNADINE BARTIE

Age 36
Insight: Yield to God

Bernadine is a busy, Spirit-filled, Word-filled preacher. In the two years since her marriage to Reverend N. C. Bartie, she has added to her previous responsibilities of raising three teenagers and holding down a full-time job, the ministries of a regular Sunday morning radio show and co-pastoring a budding new church with her husband.

Although the marriage has required many adjustments on both sides, she is happily married and thankful that God answered her prayers.

JP: How did you and your husband meet?

BB: We first met under a tent. Some friends invited me to a tent revival they were holding, and even though I was tired, I gathered the kids and we went over to hear the preaching, just to keep from being antisocial. I didn't even plan to get out of the car, but I heard the Word from the Lord coming forth and the Spirit of the Lord drew me in. Carl was delivering the message.

After the service we all went to a restaurant for coffee, and ended up talking together until 7 A.M. Since his hotel was near my apartment, my friends asked me to drop him off, but I said no because I didn't want to be seen by anyone at a hotel with a man that time of morning. I let him out at my apartment complex and he had to walk from there. He'd given me a prophecy that night, and a day or so later it came to pass, so I went back over to the tent another night to thank him. He started asking me about myself, and I invited him to my church for our revival. Even though he was supposed to be leaving town, he started to kind of follow me around and we started seeing each other.

JP: Did the Lord clue you in that this was to be your husband?

BB: Yes, He told both of us. I found out from him later that when the Lord had him call me up for the prayer and prophecy that very first night, the Lord told him, "Meet your wife."

The Lord gave me a word concerning him about two months earlier. Then, a few days after I met him, I heard the Lord say, "This is that Carl I was speaking of."

JP: Had you given up hope of marrying before this happened?

BB: I had been on my own for about eleven years and I felt like I was a veteran of the single life. There were definitely times when I gave up hope, followed by times when hope would rise up again. I went through several cycles where my hopes would be high, then after a while I'd say, "Forget it," and ask the Lord just to clear my mind and take these feelings away. But He would never do that.

I always desired to be married, to have a husband who loved the Lord and could minister with me. But it seemed like, in times past, whenever I started praying for a husband, all kinds of people would come out of the woodwork who were not of God.

I always struggled with my weight, and I had slacked up on my diet and exercise. But about a year before I met Carl, the Lord had told me to start working on myself and start losing weight because He was going to send my husband. I just left it alone because I thought it was flesh talking and I didn't want to put any hopes in the voice of the flesh. You get tired of struggling with whether God wants you to have a mate or not. You want to put your mind to something else. So I found myself not even giving in to that because I didn't want to be disappointed. I had been disappointed many times but God is faithful. In due time, if we'll be patient and faint not, He'll send us what we need.

JP: How long was it from the time you met Carl until you married?

BB: We met in July and he proposed in October, but it took till May, a total of eleven months, for the wedding to take place. It was the longest time of my life. I'd get mad at him regularly and break it off. I was ready to get married. I knew I loved him and I knew he loved me, but he still had a lot of things to deal with. The Lord had some things He was working out with him. I was the one who was always saying, "Don't worry. We can work it out."

Finally, my prayer partner and I went to work on the situation. One morning we prayed about it, and Carl told me later that same afternoon that he'd had a dream that morning in which the Lord was directing him to go ahead and get married. I smiled and told him, "Yes, we were praying about that time." After that, he was ready.

JP: Was this your second marriage?

BB: No, this is my first marriage. I feel I am a living testimony to every unwed mother, of what God can do in their lives if they just yield to Him. I have three children and had never been married. I wasn't a Christian when I had my children. In fact, my last child was born two weeks before I became a Christian.

JP: From your vantage point as a formerly unwed mom, do you have any admonitions to share?

BB: Just be very careful. There are men out there who can see when you are vulnerable. I encourage single women to have a close friend who is also walking with the Lord, a prayer partner that you can call on. Don't try to run the race alone. "In the multitude of counselors there is safety" (Prov. 11:14).

Also, be as transparent as the Lord allows you to be. Once you start hiding things, the enemy can get to you and defeat you. Be open about the feelings you are having. Stay under wise counsel. The human will, the flesh, is so strong, that if you want a thing badly enough, you can convince yourself that it's God's will. You must be careful to whom you listen. The enemy is very subtle in that area.

The Lord gave some strong warnings to me in my single life. He didn't leave me ignorant. If He gave me a word, He always gave confirmation. If I questioned Him about a man who'd come into my life, He always said, "No, this is not him." I didn't like it. I'd get upset and angry with God and have a temper tantrum, but the Spirit of God always watched over me and protected me. So yield to the Spirit. "Be steadfast, immovable, always abounding in the work of the Lord" (1 Cor. 15:58). God dealt with me several times about that Scripture, "Commit your works to the LORD, and your thoughts will be established" (Prov. 16:3). You know, once the loneliness of not having a husband or father for your kids sets in, it's hard to break that cycle in your mind. You'll get into a pity party and think God cares nothing about you.

I belonged to a singles group once and I heard the leader say something that really turned me off. She said, "We're the rejects." I refused to accept that. That thought sets you up for failure. I told the Lord, "I do not want to be single. I will not be single." But whenever the desire for a husband began to consume my thought life, God would deal with me time after time about why He still said no. It's the same as when a child doesn't understand why the parent says no. You just have to learn that He knows best.

Whenever I got involved with the church and ministry, the Lord gave me a peace about being single. I remember once, when I belonged to a different church, the pastor told a story about a woman who came up for prayer moaning, "I need a husband. I've got all these bills to pay. I need a husband." The pastor told her, "Sweetheart, you don't need a husband. You just need some money." You have to be careful because the enemy will get you into that mind-set of fantasizing about having two incomes and someone to help pay the bills. I think that's the spirit of the world. It's one of the worldly strongholds we, as Christians, still have in our minds about relationships and marriage. But being married hasn't changed that—God is still our source.

JP: So how's married life now?

BB: It's great, but God has made a lot of changes in me to get me to this point. Marriage is not what I had it to be in my carnal mind. I've had to really yield to the Spirit and hear the Spirit in my marriage, because I had some incorrect ideas that were firmly set in my mind about how the marriage relationship should be. God really dealt with me about yielding to His mind rather than my own mind-set about how it should go. I have no doubt God put us together, but our marriage, as well as our love for God, have been tested. He may still have some attitude adjustments to make, but thankfully, the major ones have been taken care of. God has given us a glimpse of what He wants to do through us. It has been an example to others in our town to see us ministering together and doing the work of the Lord, especially the work we do in the prisons. The inmates really respond to the fact that we are a husband and wife serving the Lord and ministering together.

JP: Sounds like you have a full plate. Any parting thoughts to share? What about celibacy?

BB: I would advise women to yield to God. I was a committed Christian, sanctified, and filled with the Holy Spirit, and I had a plan for my life. But it wasn't God's plan. All the time, God was trying to keep me from hurting myself. With sex before marriage, you don't even get to know each other. The first fruit of the Spirit is love and I believe God wants couples to build *philia* love first. Sex before marriage is out of order and brings all kinds of problems.

When I went ahead, at one point, and entered into a sexual relationship with a man, it seemed like every demon in the spirit realm was loosened on me. I got caught up at a time when I was very vulnerable. I had just left the church I was in over hurts I had endured there, and Satan sent this guy right on in. I was strong-willed and self-willed. I had my heart focused on the man, not on God. God had to do surgery on my mind to get him out. That's why God told the Israelites to marry within their tribe, because He didn't want them serving strange gods. It took the Lord to deliver me.

DORIS NELSON

Age 47
Insight: Use Your Faith

Doris Nelson, by the grace of God, endured a frenetic year that saw the unexpected end of her seventeen-year marriage, the onset of a life-threatening illness with its attendant surgery, followed by a surprise courtship and marriage to a deacon in her church. She has been a newlywed for a year and a half, but the insights she gained during that extraordinary time are still vivid in her memory.

JP: Tell me how you met your husband.

DN: When I met Roy I was at a really low point in my life. I was very, very sick and my marriage had just ended. All of my life I had gone to church, but I thought God had really left me. I was all alone and it seemed I had nowhere to go, that these terrible things just could not be happening to me. My life was in chaos. The doctor said I would have to have surgery to remove twelve benign tumors, but I certainly could not afford to. Who was going to take care of me? What was I going to do? I have one daughter who is a single mother with two little children and I didn't want to tell her, and I have a brother who's a Christian but I didn't want to worry him.

Then one day I got sick at work, and the doctor said, "We can't put it off any longer. We've got to do it now." Before I went into surgery, my brother came to the hospital with Roy Nelson, my sister, and some other people from the church to pray for me. Roy and my brother were friends, but I couldn't imagine why he'd bring him to pray for me because I didn't even like him. I was in the hospital for two weeks and two days.

JP: So you met when he came to the hospital?

DN: In a real way, yes. We had known each other before because he was a deacon in my church, but we never had any dealings with each other at all. We were in two opposing groups at church and didn't see eye to eye on anything. I would even say things about him that weren't really nice, even though I didn't know him. You know, we go to church and we have a tendency to judge people. In fact, I tease Roy now that this marriage might be punishment for the fact that I disliked him.

After he came to pray for me in the hospital, I found out he was someone I could talk to and enjoyed the same things I enjoyed. However, I never thought I would marry Roy Nelson, certainly not. But he's sweet, and he's good to me, and I love him, and what else did I pray and ask the Lord for? My brother says, "I know you didn't pray and ask the Lord for Roy Nelson, because I know how you used to feel about him." I tell him that I just asked the Lord to send someone into my life who could help me, someone with whom I could grow stronger in the Lord. That was what I needed. I know what the Lord has done. Every time I look at Roy, I think of how the Lord and our faith brought us together. People ask me what Roy Nelson did to make me smile so. I felt like I was seventeen years old and had gotten married for the very first time. If it ever changes, I've made a pact with the Lord that I'm going to hold Him responsible.

JP: How long were you single?

DN: For almost exactly one year. I can't even remember being single before that. I married early and it seemed I had always been married. When I became single, I discovered it was not the glamorous life I had imagined it was. It seemed that everybody else was married. I used to think that if I were single I'd go here, I would do this, and I would do that, but instead, I found myself wanting to do just the opposite. I found myself wanting to be only at home and at church. When I wasn't at church, I had nothing else I wanted to do, but that's not what single women do, I thought. The more I got involved at church and with the other singles there, I learned that just because people are single, it doesn't mean they can't praise God and be thankful just like people who are married.

I found out, though, that it's very hard to be single and a Christian. There are certain places you no longer want to go, so where do you find a single man? In a grocery store? The men are off in clubs or someplace else. It just happened that I met someone who was in the church. I never wanted to be alone. I was always afraid to take care of myself. Seventeen years is a long time to be married and then suddenly become single. When people found out I was getting divorced, they said, "But you're past forty. That's a very difficult time to be single." I felt they were right but I couldn't worry about it. If there was someone else for me, I'd get him, but I was in no hurry to marry again. I knew I didn't want to be alone for the rest of my life, but this time it was just going to have to be someone in the church. I asked for somebody who loved the Lord and who wanted to go to church, but I definitely never expected the Lord to send me a man with a position in the church; certainly not a deacon.

JP: Why? Was his position a problem?

DN: Definitely. Being single and in love with a man who was a deacon in the church was just not the best thing that could happen to a person. People acted almost like it was a crime. He was divorced and I was divorced, but a lot of people thought it was wrong.

When I got sick, people said there were all kinds of things wrong with me. They said I had tuberculosis or I had cancer. Roy felt sorry for me and came up to pray for me that night because he thought I was dying. It was really strange that he was attracted to me at all because I had been so sick that when I was able to come back to church, I didn't look good at all. I was really thin and I looked like someone whose health was failing.

When we started seeing each other, for a long, long time nobody knew for sure, and they were afraid to ask. Because Roy was a deacon, I guess he wasn't supposed to have a life. There was a lot of speculation, and things were said about us that just weren't true. I had been a member of that particular church for close to twenty years and really loved the people there, but nobody knew a lot about me and I didn't really know them. I never really knew Roy at all. If anybody thought there might have been something between us before, they actually knew better. But if you're single and a Christian, everything you do for love is wrong. I couldn't even go to Roy's house on a Saturday evening. Through our relationship I learned that if you're doing the right thing, if you're doing things that are pleasing to God, someone's wagging tongue cannot hurt you. The best thing to do is to prove those people wrong by continuing to do what you know is right. Roy and I talked about getting married as early as three months into the relationship, but that's just not how we wanted to handle it.

JP: When did you get engaged?

DN: My hospital stay was in May and he proposed in November. About a week before Thanksgiving, I was unpacking my china to put it into the china cabinet, when he knocked on the door. I had newspapers and packing material scattered all over the dining table, and Roy somehow managed to slip a box under the papers. He had just walked in and I hadn't even seen him around the table. I continued putting the glass away, then I noticed a box. I wondered out loud what that box was doing there, and he said, "Well, I guess I'd look if I were you."

It was my engagement ring, and we got married in March, almost exactly a year after my divorce.

But it really wasn't easy. I had to decide that the most important thing in my life at that point was to build a relationship with Roy. I also needed to decide if I really wanted to marry him or if I really wanted to marry a deacon. So I stayed on my knees, and one day I just knew that Roy and I could get married and have a life together. As far as other people's opinions, I learned how to look the other way and keep on smiling. The Lord had to change both of our attitudes, since Roy had only been divorced for about a year also. His divorce was devastating, and he definitely did not plan to get married again, and definitely not after only a year. That was something both of us agreed on. But we loved each other, and the life we wanted together had to be blessed by God with commitments and vows. We got married on a Friday at noon in our pastor's study. It was private and personal and very special.

JP: Do you have any insights to offer to single women?

DN: Well, one thing I would definitely say is not to accept less than you have asked the Lord for. We tend to do that, but we need to stop settling for second best because we think we're finished and nobody wants us. That's just not true. It is definitely true, however, that the older you are the harder it gets, and there's more you may have to accept. For instance, it's more likely the person you marry will have children or there'll be other things you'll have to adjust to.

I guess there was a time in my life when fancy things mattered: big two-story houses, fine cars, worldly things. But when you meet a mate, it's so important that the two of you want some of the same things. Maybe in a relationship you'll have to give up the three bathrooms and four bedrooms; can you live with that? People who knew me before look at me now and say, "Look at her. She used to live in a big fancy house. Now she lives in a little bitty house," and they'd even come up to me and say that. It hurt me because they didn't know me. Values change. Those things are material things, and I saw how much they got me. They just couldn't give me what I needed. What I needed was someone who loved me, who could help me to get through times when I needed strength, someone to lean on, who doesn't always say yes. Don't try to branch out and search for what you want. That might not be what you need. One of the analogies I like to use is if you pray and ask the Lord for a blue car but He gives you a red car, hasn't He still answered your prayer? You can leave the details up to Him.

JP: What else have you learned through all of this?

DN: I've learned to trust God. I'm just not going to worry about things that I cannot control. I worried about things for years and years. My health went to the dogs, and all the time, the Lord was right there. I knew He was there, but I would not accept that in the way that you have to accept Him in order to get through valleys. We can walk straight ahead and get through things our own way, just asking the Lord for little favors here and there. But do we know we can ask Him for big things? Until we know that, we'll never get them. I'm going to put my hopes high.

I'm at a point in my life right now where I know what the Lord has done, and I continue to hold Him accountable for more and more. Each day I get stronger and stronger, and I can tell people something good today that I wasn't able to tell them yesterday, something that can help them. I see my life going in that direction. People notice. They don't say, "Oh, here comes Doris, the preacher lady." But now they notice inner peace and smiles that are real. When I think about doing something for the glory of God, I don't consider going out there and saving somebody's life. Instead, I see the little things that might not seem important to others but they mean so much to the people you do them for. I just find myself wanting to help everybody, not in the sense of buying them a new car, but rather teaching them how to drive.

When I got out of the hospital after being so sick, I started testifying and telling people how good the Lord had been. I was surprised at how many lives my testimony touched. I found out that I had so many friends who had basically the same type of problems, but they'd been afraid to face them. I could tell them that the Lord was good and that He'd bring them through, and they would stop and listen. The same is true with my marriage to Roy. When a person's frowns turn to smiles, when the things they say to people are different, and the things they do are different, other people notice.

JP: What would you like your ultimate testimony to be?

DN: My true testimony to anyone is to hold on to and use the faith you have in God. Continue to challenge Him and ask to grow in the faith that you have. If the faith I have is the desire to do the right thing, as my faith becomes stronger, I will not only continue to do the right thing, but I'll do even better and greater things for the Lord. My faith is so strong now because I have faith and trust in the Lord. I've been through times of doubt, and I know that when the valleys come, I'll handle them even better than the last time. One thing that I really remember is something that Roy told me early in our relationship. I told him I didn't know what to pray, and he just said, "Well, I guess you've never needed something from the Lord, and you've got nothing to thank Him for." Now I never hesitate to pray. I've just really been blessed.

REBENER BRYANT

Age 40
Insight: Let Go and Let God

Every testimony up until now has provided witness to the fact that God can take us and deal with us from wherever we are, both in our personal lives and in our relationship with Him. He doesn't care where you've been, only where you are going.

This is one "strictly by the book" testimony, a living witness that it can be done God's way, all the way. Even though most of us will never travel that particular route, it is encouraging to know that it can and is still done.

Probably our least exciting testimony in a worldly sense is that of Rebener Bryant. She has no traumatic divorces, no wild ex-husbands or children to raise alone, but she does have a vibrant witness of the faithfulness of God to His Word in the life of a woman who was faithful to His Word.

JP: How did you and David meet?

RB: We lived five doors from each other. We both had a dog, and we met while walking them. I used to tease him that my dog, who weighed seventeen pounds, could beat up his dog, who was seventy pounds. But David's dog developed degenerative arthritis and had problems with his legs and spine. After a while, he couldn't walk anymore, and David had to put him down. He'd raised the dog from a puppy and had him for thirteen years, and he felt really badly about it. He was grieving and needed a friendly ear, so one evening he came over to my apartment and knocked on the door at 10 P.M. I actually let him in. We talked for a couple of hours, then he went home.

We became really good friends. He's the kind of person you meet and immediately feel as if you've known him for a long time. If you needed to talk to a friend in the middle of the night you could always go to him. He always had friends in his apartment, visiting and watching athletic events on television.

Shortly after we became friends he started going to my church, and we would talk for hours about the Lord.

JP: Was he a Christian?

RB: Yes, but he was looking for a church. No, actually he was looking in the church for a wife. We would talk about that sometimes too. One evening he came up and was telling me how he'd gone to church looking for his wife, and how he would usually see a woman and think, "Maybe this is the one, Lord," so he'd go up and introduce himself. He'd be disappointed when she'd say, "Hi, how are you?" and go on about her business. While we were talking about this I told him, "You shouldn't go to church to look for a wife; you should go to church to find God." I remember him looking at me real strange, and suddenly he had to go home. It was like he'd suddenly gotten sick or something, and he had to leave right then. I wondered what had happened.

Later on, he told me that when I said that his eyes opened and the Lord said to him, "This is your wife." He had to go home and talk to the Lord. He told Him, "She is not my wife—she's my friend." He went back and forth with the Lord about that but he didn't win. A couple of weeks later he told me what the Lord had said. I was not at all prepared for this, so I told him, "If I was your wife, the Lord would have told me first before He told you." I felt I would know before he would know because I was more spiritual.

So he agreed to remain just friends. David was very patient with me. He knew what the Lord had told him, and he waited patiently for two years before I came around. The Lord just left the decision up to me. It was as if He said, "Rebener, this is your decision. I'm not saying a word to you." I believe the Lord trusted me enough to make the right decision. I was following certain biblical and family guidelines, and I guess He agreed that if I followed those, I was going to make the right choice.

Things slowly started happening to open my eyes and change my mind. For instance, at the time I didn't have a car and David would take me back and forth to work. One day when I arrived at work, one of the ladies in the office wanted to know who he was. I told her all about how nice he was and how he was like my best friend, and she asked, "Why don't you marry him?" I was surprised by this and I said, "He's my friend." She said, "You should marry your best friend." That stuck with me, even though at the time I thought, "No way."

After a while though, he started pushing me to get married, so I had to stop to think about my criteria, and if he met them. One of my main prayers, when I had prayed and asked the Lord for a husband was, "Lord, I want this, and that, and that. But You know me and what I need. You know my personality and the man who's best suited for me. You choose the husband." I got that from my mother because she always told me she had let God choose her husband, and I always thought I had the most wonderful daddy in the world. He died when I was ten, but we had some wonderful times together. So I was determined I was going to let God do the choosing. He knows you on the inside better than anybody else, and when you get married, what's on the inside is going to come out.

JP: What were your criteria?

RB: Well, I asked for a tall, slender man, but David has medium height and a heavy build. I asked for a jack-of-all-trades, and David does a little bit of everything. I didn't want a minister or a lawyer and David is neither. I wanted a very clean and meticulous man but David is messy. In fact, his mother told me, "If he's anything like his father, you'll have junk in your house for the rest of your life." I wanted a man who loved children, and David and his family are the most children-loving people I've ever met. He is very caring, loving, and kind. And although I didn't know it at the time, I also needed a patient man, which David has definitely shown himself to be.

I also wanted a man who believed in the Lord Jesus Christ. That was one of my major concerns, and I wanted us to be members of the same church. David would go to my church every Sunday, but he just would not join. He did pray, and I could talk freely to him about the gifts of God and the fruit of the Spirit, and he was open to them, but my church was really different for him. They always told us in the singles ministry to make sure a man's been a Christian for at least a year before you marry him. David finally decided to join, and he had been a member for a little over a year when we got married. So everything just worked out.

JP: How old were you when you married?

RB: I was thirty-eight, and David was thirty-seven.

JP: Was this your first marriage?

RB: It was the first one for both of us. I had been engaged twice before but they didn't work out. However, my first question to David was, "Why haven't you ever gotten married before?" I wanted to know what was wrong with him. That's always the first thing a guy wants to know. Are you married? Have you ever been married? And, how many children do you have? They don't seem to understand if you're over thirty, never married, and without children. So the tables got kind of turned when I wanted to know why he had never married nor had children.

JP: Had you been praying for a husband?

RB: Not really. I was never worried or concerned about it. I see that as a big difference between me and a lot of single women who are always worrying about it, always praying about it. Whenever I would think about it, I would pray about it then drop it. I would hear women saying, "I'm going to be married by such and such a time," but I was never concerned about that. What concerned me was that I wanted to be happy, and I knew if I got married and I wasn't happy, I would leave the marriage. I planned to do this only one time, so I was willing to take my time. I knew that it was very important to be happy in a marriage and satisfied with the mate you have.

As preparation for marriage I also started going to the excellent women's Bible study we had at church. I started looking at different women around the church who had really good marital relationships. I'm a watcher of people, and I would sit back and observe how they interacted with their husbands, with other people, even with children. As women, we are generally not taught how to be good wives and good mothers. I was taught how to work hard, how to get an education, and how to stay out of trouble. But I was not taught what to expect in a marriage. When I realized my ignorance about marriage, I wanted to find out as much as I could. So I began to pay close attention to those things.

Another thing that I did, when I decided I was ready to marry, was to ask the Lord what I needed to do next. He said, "Go to your singles ministers (who were a married couple), and tell them that you want a husband, that you're ready to get married." I really didn't want to do that but I was obedient. When I told the wife she asked, "What do you want in a husband?" I didn't expect that question and didn't have an answer, but she started naming off all these things I should be asking for, and I was nodding my head, saying, "Yes, I want that. And I want that too." Then she prayed for me, called her husband over, and said, "Guess what? Rebener is ready to get married." He got excited, and they prayed a wonderful prayer for me together. About nine months later, I met David.

JP: Can I ask you your opinion on celibacy?

RB: Oh, definitely yes. If you want a good marriage, that has to come first. One of the ways I knew David respected me was that he respected my opinion on sex before marriage. If you meet a man who doesn't try to change your mind, or give you reasons why you should, then even if you never get married, you've got a good friend.

Once I had a group of women over and we were talking in general, when one woman said she was looking to marry and the Lord had told her, "You've got to stop having sex with men if you want a husband." I feel very strongly that is true. I believe I received more revelation knowledge directly from God, because I abstained from sex. I always felt if a man wanted my body and didn't want to marry me, he could forget it. The two go hand in hand.

JP: How long were you celibate?

RB: For over ten years. I would like single women to know that you can live without a man; you can really do it. It's all in giving everything over to the Lord. Just give Him a chance.

I had attended church all my life, but the dedication of my life to God did not come about until He decided to tell me what He had allowed me to do, and that now it was time for me to live for Him. He spoke to me on three different occasions, showing me things in both my childhood and adulthood that He had allowed in my life. Then He said, "Now it's My turn. It's time for you to serve Me."

JP: Do you have any admonitions to pass along to single women?

RB: Have patience, patience, and more patience. And when you pray, act like the Lord heard you. The Scriptures tell us to keep on knocking, keep on seeking, but it's important not to act like you're desperate. If you get out there and you're acting desperate, Satan looks at you and puts stumbling blocks in your way. I never acted desperate, and I never felt desperate. That's very important. There is no need to—your husband is out there.

You may need to ask the Lord to open his eyes so he can see you, because that way you won't go out there and get in the Lord's way.

Another thing is to be friendly. I didn't know if David was Christian or not when I met him, but I was friendly. Even if you're going to witness to someone, you need to have a friendly attitude. Be hospitable. My apartment was always open to people in need, single mothers, or even couples. I enjoyed cooking for people and would invite single male friends who didn't cook for themselves for dinner once in a while. I didn't expect anything in return, but if you're friendly, whenever you need a friend you'll have a friend, and you never know when you'll need somebody.

Holidays can be times of depression for a single person, but it can be different if you learn to practice hospitality and establish your own traditions. I would go out and find people who were going to be alone, or had no place to spend Christmas, or no money or whatever, and I would cook a great big Christmas dinner and invite all these people over. They weren't all Christians, and they included people of all races and backgrounds. The first year I did that, two people became Christians. Their Christian walk began as a result of an act of hospitality and friendliness.

By being friendly, you'll also have people to go out and do things with. I used to go roller-skating with my next-door neighbor. There were other people I would walk or jog with. That way you don't get lonely. Keep yourself busy, not just doing things for yourself but for other people as well. Grandmother used to say, "Idle hands are the devil's workshop." I went to school and took some classes, was active in my church, and put in a lot of overtime on my job, so I had a full life and no time to worry about being married.

Stay close to your family, provided you've got a family that you want to stay close to. When you get ready to make a very big decision in your life, allow them to help you make that decision. If you have brothers or uncles, they can give you that male input and sometimes that can really help. If you're not close to your family, get input from someone in the church.

JP: Rebener, I remember your wedding being particularly beautiful. What has happened since?

RB: Thank you for the compliment. Two weeks after our wedding David's dad died, and a month after that, he got laid off and was out of work for a year. This was also the time when I began to experience symptoms of illness. I went through many tests, and eventually the doctors confirmed that I had a pituitary adenoma, a brain tumor. On the X rays, there was a growth attached to my pituitary gland that was the size of a fifty-cent piece, while my pituitary gland was the size of a green pea. We prayed for my healing and when the doctor cut through my skull and saw the growth, he stuck a needle in it, and it popped like a bubble. That was all it was. I spent less than twenty-four hours in ICU.

Through that trial, the Lord showed me how patient David really was. Going through that struggle with him was a real blessing. He is very special. He's that patient person I did not know to ask the Lord for when I was single. He was that "You know what I need, Lord." He really put up with a lot and I thank God for him.

JP: What would you like your ultimate testimony to be?

RB: That you must let go and let God. Let Him do it. He knows everything about you, and He knows everything about that man. He knows where he is and what he's doing. Maybe the reason you don't have a husband yet is that God needs to prepare the man for you. Instead of you needing to be prepared, perhaps God still has some work to do in him.

Don't get in front of God. Don't go ahead of Him and try to do it yourself. Let God do it for you. He knows what He is doing. It's in His perfect timing. If I had gotten married before the time that we should have married, I would have been divorced because I would have married the wrong man.

CYNDI STEWART

Age 36
Insight: Focused and Faithful

From the very beginning, I knew that this next testimony had to be included. Cyndi is the single woman who has been a very special inspiration for this book. Our friendship began eight years ago, while I was also single and struggling to live a godly life. She'll never know just how much her example positively influenced my decisions.

Because she is still single, I almost submitted to the tyranny of format and excluded her testimony, but as I have stated from the first page of this book, this is not my book. God knew the impact of her story, even when I had concluded that all the bases had been covered. As you read on, you'll understand why this, His book, would have been incomplete without the testimony of this exceptional woman of God.

JP: How long have you been a Christian?

CS: I don't know exactly. I can't say it was back in 1980, or how many years it has been. Probably fifteen to twenty years. I remember growing up knowing about God and having my grandmother read the Bible to me, but I was a teenager before I realized who God is and who He is in my life. My parents didn't go to church regularly, but I sought it out. I had a girlfriend in junior high school who went to church every Sunday. She sang in the choir and was very involved in the church, and I was intrigued by that. Her mother would pick me up sometimes and I would go to church with them. That is the church my parents go to today, because I encouraged them to go.

JP: How long have you been single?

CS: I've been single for ten years.

JP: How long were you married, and was your husband a Christian?

CS: I was married for only three and a half years, and no, he wasn't a Christian.

JP: Was that a reason for the breakup of the marriage?

CS: I'm sure it played a part. We were young when we got married. He got baptized during the time we were married but that was for me. It wasn't because of his relationship with God. He was not brought up in a Christian home, and I realized after we got married, that he really had no idea what I was talking about when I would talk about church, or Christianity, or prayer, or any of that. After a while, it began to bother him that every Sunday I would get up and go to church. He would always get upset and want to know, "Why can't you stay home with me today?" At first I did. In my mind, I was bargaining with him, which meant there would be some Sundays when he would get up and go with me to church. Then I realized I was compromising in the wrong direction. If he didn't ever want to go, that was fine, but I couldn't let him stop the progress I was making just because he didn't understand and didn't want to go.

JP: Do you date now?

CS: No, and I don't know why. As much as I'm out and as busy as I am, you would think I would have met someone, but there just has not been anyone I've wanted to date. I'm grateful God keeps me focused and not anxious. There have been several interested men, but dating hasn't happened. But a couple of close friendships have resulted. He keeps me very busy with other things and I like that. A lot of people ask me, "Oh, you're so attractive and intelligent. Why don't you date?" That's funny to me because I don't think those attributes are criteria—I don't think every attractive, intelligent woman out there is dating. I'd really feel left out if that were the case. I think that when you turn your life over to God things just happen differently. I've gotten to the point where I don't really dwell on it.

Dating means different things to different people, and to me it means caring and sharing; having a person who cares about me, who has my best interest in mind, who cares about my daughter, who cares about things we do and how we're doing. That's dating to me, especially at my age. I don't need someone just to take me to a movie or to dinner. If I want to go to a movie, I can spend ten bucks and take myself. To me, dating is a relationship with a person who cares for me, respects me, shares common ideals with me. I think that dating in that sense is wonderful.

JP: Do you have a time frame for marriage?

CS: No. I just don't want to wake up one morning at seventy-three, look over on the other side of the bed, and find it empty and cold. I'd like to get married. I'd like to build a relationship, but as far as a time frame, I think a lot of women do that because they want to have children. That's not an issue with me. There are a lot of things I want to do with my life. I'm not waiting for a man to make me better, or make me complete, or to buy me a house, or give me other things. There are some goals I've set to accomplish and I don't necessarily want to accomplish them by myself, but it just so happens that that's the way it is right now.

If I were married it would be fine, but I'm not and it's okay. I don't need to be married by the time I'm forty or forty-three, or by the time my daughter gets to be a certain age. It's just whenever the time comes. A lot of people get caught up in age but I'm not one of those people. I don't let the number of my age dictate who I am, or how I should feel, or where I should be in life, because I think that's different for everybody. So I don't think at thirty-five you need to be here and at forty you need to be there. I think you need to be wherever God has you. This is where He has me right now and I'm excited to be in His will, doing things according to His timetable. He has given me goals, aims, and ambitions, and I'm grateful because I feel that I have a vision from heaven. I'm looking forward to building my life and seeing what the world has to offer. I feel like my life now is an adventure with God, and my daughter, Lauren, is learning and exploring with me. I want her to be open to trying things and going places, observing and discerning her surroundings to see what's out there. To me, you can much better pick and choose when you know what you're picking and choosing from. The more you know, the more intelligent are the choices you can make.

I have no time line. Whenever it's time, I'll be okay with it. I don't know if it's soon or not, but I have a lot of ideas about getting married. I have ideas about my wedding, about the person, about the life, but I have no idea when it's going to happen.

JP: Are these ideas that you have or has God given you a vision of them?

CS: I'm sure it is a combination of both. I have ideas about the kind of person I want to marry and the kind of life I want us to lead. I don't want to marry just anybody. My friends tell me I'm too picky. I don't know if picky is a good term but I am very selective. If you aim high, you may not get to the stars, but you'll be a lot higher than if you don't. So I may aim very, very high but I think I leave a lot of the riffraff down below, because I've aimed past that. There may be only a small selection of people in my aiming sight but I only need one. Hopefully, whoever I'm united with will have aimed high also, because I see myself as an interesting, intelligent, attractive, articulate person, and somewhat adventurous; and that's the kind of person I'd like to marry and spend the rest of my life living, loving, and learning with.

JP: Are you actively seeking a husband?

CS: No. If you hadn't said "actively," I could have answered you better. Active means something I'm doing. I'm not sure I'm actively doing it. The second thing is that I'm not seeking a husband. In praying about a mate, God has let me know that I don't have to seek or look for a husband. When He's ready to provide me a husband, it'll just be done. I won't have to look for him. Friends say to me, "Why don't you come to this party or to that function, because there'll be single men there." But if I decide not to go to that function, I don't think I'll miss meeting my husband, because wherever I'm supposed to be, when the time comes I'll be there. I won't miss it if I'm in tune with the lead and direction of the Holy Spirit. God will not let me miss what He has in store for me. It takes the worry and the labor out of it. Don't get me wrong. It's like anything else. If I want something, or in this case, somebody, there are certain things I have to do. If I want a husband, there is a certain amount of effort I must make but only God knows who he is and where he is, so I'll depend on God to lead me.

JP: What are some of the things that you have to do?

CS: I have to know what I want, so that when I meet a man I can discern if this could even be him, because I know what I want and what I've asked for. I'll also have to be very prayerful. Just like anything else, God will let me know if this is it, even if it doesn't seem right to me at the time. There are a lot of times that God will do something, and I'll kind of look back out the corner of my eye and think, "Do You really mean this?" But He lets me know, "Yes, I do really mean this." And I go on, even though this is not what I would have planned. It doesn't matter that I understand it. The fact that I know it's from God is enough. I just know that whatever I need to know, when I need to know it, He'll tell me. I would like to think that my relationship with Him is strong enough and close enough that I'll recognize Him when He speaks and be obedient to what He says.

JP: Do you have a list of attributes that you are praying for in a mate?

CS: Yes, I do. I don't know that all of them have come from God, but knowing me and the things I like, I know what I'd like to have in a husband. But I trust that God will always do better than I can ever ask, so even if I give Him this list that I think is absolutely wonderful, He can send me somebody better than that. I believe we can't even envision what God has in store for us, so I try not to limit Him. As I said before, it's important to me that the man be active and involved. It's also important to me that the man is tall. That's just one of the things I like in men. It's important to me that he is giving and that he has a family orientation. I think that if you have a sense of family, when you get a family you'll have a much better sense of what that's all about in the true sense of family; that is, what it means to care, to give, to share, to love, and to support.

Those are things I would like to have in a husband. I also want someone who will absolutely adore my daughter, simply because she is adorable and she deserves to be adored. And the same thing with me. I think I have a lot to bring to a relationship, and out there is some man who will appreciate the qualities I bring.

JP: Has God spoken to you regarding a husband?

CS: Yes. A husband has not been a priority for me. I've enjoyed my life and I enjoy being single. However, I was praying one day a few months ago, asking God to direct my prayer life. I said, "God, You know what You're going to do. You direct my prayer life to pray in Your will, according to Your will. I don't know what to pray for. You direct me. Tell me what I'm to pray for because You know what You're going to do in my life and I want to pray according to that." I didn't expect to get an answer right then, but He really surprised me because He immediately named three things I was to pray for, right there while I was still on my knees: a mate, a move, and a career change.

At the time I said, "Well, God, I'll pray for these things; but I like where I live; there is nowhere for me to go at my job, and I like what I do already; and a mate, that's a real big question mark. But, because You're God, I'll pray about them." That was the first time He's told me anything about a mate. It may have been the first time I was open enough to hear Him say that but it was like I had said, "Okay, You pour into this empty cup whatever You want it filled with," and those are the things He filled my cup with that morning. I have been praying about them since then and I know I'm to pray about them until they come to pass. And at the end of this month, I'm moving.

Whenever I prayed about these things with my prayer partner, I had been focusing on the career change I believe He is directing me to make within the next year. I told her, "While we're praying about this, I don't want to miss praying about . . . ," and before I could say "the move and the mate," the Holy Spirit just broke in and said, "This is your move. You're moving according to My plan." I had been questioning the move I was considering because it didn't fit in with the next logical step in my own thinking, but it does with God's divine way of thinking. And He just kind of birthed it into my spirit.

It's so awesome that you can talk to God and God talks back to you and allows you to see His hand at work. It's wonderful to know that God's plan is being worked out in your life. So whatever happens, God is not going to sit up in heaven with His hands over His face saying, "Oh my goodness, I did not know that was going to happen. Had I known that I would never have let you do it." He knows it all, so whatever happens just do it, just follow Him. I pray to stay in His plan and His will, that I don't go before Him or resist Him, just because I may not like what He wants or feel comfortable with it. I pray that I always know and that He always affirms for me that, "Yes, you're still in the plan; you haven't deviated or gotten out of sync with Me."

JP: That comes from having an active prayer life.

CS: Yes, and it's so natural for me. I talk to God like I'm talking to you. I don't make it some big ritual; I just do it. It's not your traditional down-on-your-knees communication. But, there are times that I feel if I don't bow down before Him, I'm just not fit, that the least I can do is to bow down before my Lord and King. But there are other times that I just want to talk to Him because He's my Everything. He's my Friend, and I treat Him like my friend and just sit down and talk to Him. Then, there are those times when He's my God and my King, and I want to worship Him and kneel at His feet. Sometimes He's my Comforter, and I want to tell Him all the stuff that's going on, and how I want to be healed and helped through all of this. I guess it's according to where I am and who He is to me at that particular time that determines how I pray. But, there's not a day that goes by that I don't pray. It's like any other relationship. You have to work at it, you have to talk. You can't miss that communication time or you'll miss that closeness.

JP: Let me ask you about celibacy. How long have you been celibate?

CS: You know, I don't know that either because it wasn't planned. I've never sat down and told God, "Because I'm a Christian I want to be celibate." At least I don't remember saying that. I do remember years ago, maybe seven or eight years, I had a male friend over and we almost made love—no, we almost had sex. But I remember thinking how awful that made me feel. The next day was Sunday, and I remember telling God at the altar, "I don't ever want to feel like that again, and if You will help me with this, I would like to dedicate that part of my life to the way You would like to run it." I realized it was an area I hadn't turned over to God but it wasn't that precise or focused. I just knew that what I felt the night before I didn't ever want to feel again, to be with somebody I wasn't in love with when it wasn't all of the things it was supposed to be.

So I do remember praying that, but I don't know if the celibacy started then or not. It feels so natural for me. There have been men that I cared a lot about, even some who have actually spent the night in my home. But it had to be from God. There is no way an adult woman can let an adult man spend the night and tell him, "I will not have sex and you need to understand that," and everything is fine. That is so out of character for men, and so against their nature, but God can change that. I don't do it just to test God. It's not like standing out in the street daring a Mack truck to hit me because I've prayed prior to that. My celibacy is just something that has happened and I'm very grateful for that. When I was starting out, I didn't know why I was saying no, but now I know it's the course God has me on. I joke that God must be saving me for some evangelist or something, but I figure whatever He's saving me for, it's good, because God doesn't do anything that's not good. And it hasn't been a problem for me. It's not hard for me at all, and that, too, has to be from God. Even with men I've cared a great deal about, my commitment to God is stronger than any other commitment I could make. I've just decided that, "If this is what You want for me, this is what I want for me too, so strengthen me to handle it." And He has.

JP: He didn't just stop sending guys your way?

CS: No, and I'm glad of that, because I think I would have misunderstood it if men stopped finding me attractive. I would have been thinking that maybe the reason I'm not having anybody to say "no" to is because nobody wants me to say yes to them. But the men have been there and His answer has been the same. It's very important to me to become the friend of the man I will marry, and I think that when you have sex you cloud the friendship. It's hard to develop the true and honest friendship that's required. I think sex is the icing on the cake but you have to bake the cake first. That's the friendship, the relationship, knowing one another and what the person likes and dislikes, how he feels about things, his sensitivities, and if he is easily provoked. The lovemaking part comes anyway, but the other parts of the relationship don't just happen. You need to make sure you have the cake before you try to ice it.

JP: Do you have any advice or admonitions to pass on to other single Christian women?

CS: Just to stay focused and faithful to God because He will always stay faithful to you. Whatever it is that you want, that you aim for, whatever your strengths or weaknesses, you can always go to God with all of that. Those strengths and weaknesses make up who you are, and there's a process to becoming who God wants you to be. Be open to that process.

First, you have to make up your mind that you really want to become who God wants you to be, because we often really don't want to be anything other that what we are. We like that. There was a time when I had to be in control, to show others that I could handle myself. I used sarcasm for that but God showed me that I didn't need that, that He's in control, and He knows what is best. How can I be in control when I can see only the little picture? A year from now, the choice I would have made today could be totally wrong and only He knows what's going to happen. You have to let Him guide every situation. Staying focused on and faithful to God will touch every aspect of your life.

Another thing I've realized is that we need to share more. It doesn't have to be financial sharing—share your time.

There are so many people in need. I'm extremely blessed in that I have a caring and loving family and friends, so even though I'm raising a daughter alone, we never feel alone. But there are a lot of people, including children, who feel so alone. And there are a lot of adults who have time, money, talents, and everything else to give, and they don't. To me, every time you have something to give and you don't share it, somebody is missing out on a blessing. I think that's a problem.

I've asked God, "What can I do? I know there are needs out there and some of them are huge. I will never be able to touch those, but show me the ones I can do something about." I've decided, in my limited capacity, there is still something I can do. I plan to become a volunteer at a nearby shelter for the homeless, and I have a bundle of clothes I'm taking over there on Sunday. I chose Sunday so that my daughter can go with me because I want her to see that all children don't live like she does. I get tired of hearing people say what they would do, but do nothing, because if you do nothing you're not even scratching the surface. Scratching the surface is okay, because at least you're doing something. If you only talk, nothing happens.

God has opened up my mind and it's wonderful. I feel like I'm on an adventure with God. I don't have to worry about where we're going or if there will be a shipwreck. It reminds me of that passage in Scripture where the disciples were in the boat and they woke Jesus up and asked, "Don't You care?" We look at that now and think, "Oh, how could they?" But you would do it too. You'd wonder, "Why isn't He doing something about this?" But in that same passage, Jesus told them, "Let us cross over to the other side" (Mark 4:35). They were already scheduled to make it to the other side, and we tend to miss that. He didn't say there wasn't going to be a storm in the middle, but He did get them to the other side. So I just kind of rest in that. God is guiding me, and storms will arise and I may get confused, but I just pray to stay focused and to trust that no matter what happens my eyes stay on God and not on the circumstances, and that I know He is in control.

JP: What would you like your ultimate testimony to be?

CS: I would like for other people to look at me and be able to say, "That's what happens when you let God lead your life." I'd like my life to be an example of what happens when you allow God to control you. I believe that when God blesses you, He does not bless you for you alone. He blesses you so others can see what trusting in God does. Even when things are bad and your back is up against the wall, people are looking to see if all that God-talk you've done will sustain you in a crisis. What do you do? How do you handle it?

Once again, we need to stay focused on God. We really don't know who is watching us, but during any struggle, somebody may come up to you and say, "It is amazing how you're handling this." And you will give the glory to God. Later, when that person goes through a struggle, she'll remember that. Your struggles are not always for you; sometimes they are, sometimes they aren't, but it's not our concern to know what God is doing and why. Our concern is to respond to and handle situations as God wants us to. Whether or not I ever marry is not the important issue. My relationship with God is. He'll take care of everything else.

Epilogue

It has been a long, hopefully enlightening and entertaining journey to this point. If you have been attending to the necessities outlined in Parts 1, 2, and 3, your very own miracle should be near at hand. If you have not, the next move is up to you. God will wait patiently until you are ready to proceed.

You can anticipate encountering lots of fun, excitement, and work along the way, but the reward will be well worth the effort. Just don't forget that as the women in Part 4 have so vividly pointed out, once you have met and wed the man you are dreaming of, your journey will only have begun.

Next comes the task of living with him in the context of Christian marriage. Although it will be a challenge to you both, the presence of the Holy Trinity will help to ease the rough spots and keep you focused on the big picture. Please take these testimonies you have read to heart and don't try to reinvent the wheel. God's rules are absolutes and the consequences are guarantees. You may not be able to follow His plan to the letter, but your earnest attempt to do so will be amply rewarded.

SPREAD THE WORD

When you have succeeded and God has given you the desire of your heart, don't just take your guy and run. Get out there and spread the word. It is your responsibility as a

Christian to tell others what God has done. In Mark 5:19, Jesus instructs a man for whom He has worked a miracle to, "Go home to your friends, and tell them what great things the Lord has done for you, and how He has had compassion on you." King David, in Psalm 26:7 vowed to God that he would "proclaim with the voice of thanksgiving, and tell of all Your wondrous works."

God is blessed by the testimonies of His people who tell others of His love and willingness to answer prayers. If He has shown Himself faithful in your life, be faithful to Him also. There are many single women you will meet who need the encouragement only you and your special example can provide. You can help to defeat the spirits of depression, despair, and hopelessness that are always waiting to attack Single Christian Women. But please don't wait until that husband prayer has been answered. God hears and responds to you every day in countless ways, large and small. You already have many testimonies to share with others. Don't be stingy with your praise of God.

UNTIL THEN

Continue to abide by God's Word and make the most of the life He has given you. Relax and be confident in your Lord—He knows what He is doing. Our final Scripture, which you have probably already committed to memory, is "I can do all things through Christ who strengthens me" (Phil. 4:13). Now let's take it deep into our hearts and put some legs on it. If you walk that verse every day, you'll never again be the same. Your potential is all there and all things are possible.

All praise and glory be to God.